GW00818702

STUDENT INTERACTIVE MULTIMEDIA IN
A COMPONENT OF

MARKETING

AN INTERACTIVE LEARNING SYSTEM

DAVID E. HARTMAN, Ph.D
D. HARTMAN ASSOCIATES
CHARLOTTESVILLE, VA

JOHN H. LINDGREN, JR.
UNIVERSITY OF VIRGINIA

TERENCE A. SHIMP
UNIVERSITY OF SOUTH CAROLINA

THE DRYDEN PRESS
HARCOURT BRACE COLLEGE PUBLISHERS

Fort Worth Philadelphia San Diego New York Orlando Austin San Antonio
Toronto Montreal London Sydney Tokyo

Copyright © 1996 by Harcourt Brace & Company

All rights reserved. No part of this publication may be reproduced or transmitted in any form or by any means, electronic or mechanical, including photocopy, recording or any information storage and retrieval system, without permission in writing from the publisher.

Although for mechanical reasons all pages of this publication are perforated, only those pages imprinted with a Harcourt Brace & Company copyright notice are intended for removal.

Requests for permission to make copies of any part of the work should be mailed to: Permissions Department, Harcourt Brace & Company, 6277 Sea Harbor Drive, Orlando, FL 32887-6777.

Address for Orders
The Dryden Press
6277 Sea Harbor Drive
Orlando, FL 32887-6777
1-800-782-4479 or 1-800-433-0001 (in Florida)

Address for Editorial Correspondence
The Dryden Press
301 Commerce Street, Suite 3700
Fort Worth, TX 76102

ISBN: 0-03-018112-7

Printed in the United States of America

5 6 7 8 9 0 1 2 3 4 023 9 8 7 6 5 4 3 2 1

The Dryden Press
Harcourt Brace College Publishers

Table of Contents

Introduction

Welcome to SIMIS!

SIMIS–Student Interactive Multimedia Instructional System–is an interactive principles of marketing learning program that puts you, the student, in charge of learning. By taking advantage of the latest multimedia technology, SIMIS provides the tools to page through text interactively; explore videos and print ads that illustrate marketing principles; take notes electronically; and interact with chapter review questions that automatically recall relevant text when needed.

Additionally, at the beginning of each chapter you can review the profile of an industry leader–Captains of Industry–and become familiar with a case illustration of the chapter's topics–Marketing Highlights. Other features include an extensive glossary of terms, the ability to print screens and notes, and interact with text sensitive material. SIMIS promises a rewarding educational experience.

SIMIS, through multimedia technology, presents educational material in multiple formats making it a powerful learning tool. Fred T. Hofstetter (1995) *Multimedia Literacy*, recognized that "people retain only 20% of what they see and 30% of what they hear. But they remember 50% of what they see *and* hear, and as much as 80% of what they see, hear and do *simultaneously.*"

Students who do not have access to the SIMIS CD-ROM still have an excellent educational experience available to them through the use of *Marketing: An Interactive Learning System* by John H. Lindgren, Jr. and Terence A. Shimp in combination with this SIMIS manual. Specific suggestions for book and manual users will be made in the Study Suggestions Section later in this chapter to ensure effective use of the educational material.

Copyright © 1996 by Harcourt Brace & Company
All rights reserved.

Getting Started

System Requirements

The minimum computer requirements to operate SIMIS are:

Multimedia PC or equivalent (486 or higher)
Windows 3.1
Super VGA 256 video controller
8MB RAM
MPC Compatible CD-ROM driver
Audio Board
Hard drive.

Program Installation

Installation of SIMIS is an easy process that will take just a minute. The setup process installs the SIMIS icon on the hard drive, which requires very little hard drive space. The program itself runs completely off the CD-ROM. A SIMIS icon will appear on the Windows Program Manager screen in a program group called Project SIMIS. SIMIS operates in the Windows environment and its menu bar follows all of the Windows conventions.

To install the SIMIS program, complete the following steps:

1. Open the Windows Program Manager
2. Insert the SIMIS CD in the CD-ROM drive.
   The CD-ROM drive is usually the D drive.
3. Choose File Run from the Windows Program Manager menu.
4. Type *d:\setup* in the Command Line text box.
   If the CD-ROM is in a drive other than D, substitute d:\ with the proper drive notation.
5. Click OK.
   SIMIS will perform the installation procedures.

Copyright © 1996 by Harcourt Brace & Company
All rights reserved.

> **SIMIS Tip**
> Screen savers are generally incompatible with SIMIS. For best results, make sure that all screen savers are turned off.

Starting Instructions

Open the Windows Program Manager if it was closed after the installation procedure.

1. Open the SIMIS Program group.
2. Double click the SIMIS icon.

    SIMIS will load the basic program into your operating system and display the SIMIS logo.
3. Click the Start Button to open a Bookmark dialog box and the Table of Contents.
4. Click once on the chapter title in the left-hand column to choose the chapter in which you are interested.
5. Click twice on the section name in the right-hand column to navigate directly to a section of interest in the chosen chapter.

> **SIMIS Tip**
> If you are having trouble with fuzzy or distorted pictures in SIMIS, check for other programs that are running simultaneously, such as a resident program running in the background. Other programs often cause a color palette shift that leads to the picture distortion.

Bookmark

When the Start Button is clicked, a Bookmark dialog box appears. To whether you have used this application (SIMIS program) before and whether you saved a Bookmark file. If you

Copyright © 1996 by Harcourt Brace & Company
All rights reserved.

saved and would like to recall the earlier file, click the Yes Button, otherwise click the No Button.

After you have completed reading a section, the SIMIS Bookmark places a check mark in front of the section title int he Table of Contents. When you exit SIMIS, another dialog box appears and asks whether you would like to save the Bookmark. A default file name (bookmark.txt) and disk drive (A) are offered. You may change either or both to suit your purposes. If you change the file name, retain the "txt" suffix, which is required for program recognition.

If a Bookmark file was saved and is recalled at the beginning of the next SIMIS session, the section check marks will appear in front of the sections that were read.

SIMIS Tip

Dedicating one floppy disk to the SIMIS program is a good practice. The disk will be useful for storing Bookmark information and Notepad data, which will be discussed later in this chapter.

Windows Menu

The menu bar across the top of the screen–in conformity to the Windows convention–offers the following choices: File, Edit, Section, Page, Tools, and Help.

SIMIS Tip
To shorten the learning curve, open the SIMIS program and explore the menu items and navigation tools while reading these instructions.

4

Copyright © 1996 by Harcourt Brace & Company
All rights reserved.

File

File contains three options–Print Setup, Print Pages, and Exit. Print Setup allows the selection of the desired printer for printing SIMIS screens. The available printer choices are those that have been included in the Windows program.

Use Print Pages to print the current SIMIS screen. When this option is clicked, a Print Pages dialog box appears with the question, "Print current page?" Click OK to print the screen that you are currently viewing. Make sure that you printer is turned on

The Exit option closes the SIMIS program.

Edit

The functions that are available under the Edit choice are Disable Background Music and Find. Background music is played when the review questions at the end of the chapter are accessed. The music can be turned off with the Disable Background Music option from the Review Questions section.

Find is a search function that locates words throughout the SIMIS program. A dialog box opens when the Find option is clicked. Enter a word of interest in the dialog box and click Find. The program will open the page that contains the first occurrence of the word and will highlight the position of the word on the page. The dialog box may have to be dragged to another position on the screen to see the highlighted word. Click Find Next to locate the next occurrence of the word or click Close to exit the find function.

Section

The options in the Section menu may be used to navigate through a chapter. The Next and Previous options move the user forward or backward one section at a time. (The right Arrow Button and Left Arrow Button also move the user forward and backward one

Copyright © 1996 by Harcourt Brace & Company
All rights reserved.

section at a time.) The First and Last options move the user to the first section or the last section of the chapter.

Page

Page includes options to move though the pages of text within a chapter section. The Up and Down options move the user one page at a time. The Top and Bottom options move the user to the beginning or end of the text. The Back option recalls the screen that was viewed immediately prior to the present screen. The History option lists the screens viewed during the current session. In the History option double click the screen of choice to return to a screen viewed at an earlier time of the current session.

Features

Features includes two options, Captains of Industry and Marketing Highlights. When one of these options is selected, the complete portfolio of the tool becomes available and the user may navigate through the portfolio by using the Right Arrow Button or the Left Arrow Button. The Return Button recalls the screen that was on view at the time the Tool option was selected.

Help

Help contains the options Glossary, Bibliography, About Tool Bar, About Marketing . . . . The Glossary option opens a screen of marketing terms that are sorted in alphabetical order. The scroll bar may be used to view additional terms. Click on a term to view its definition. The definitions of marketing terms may also be accessed by clicking Hotwords as they appear in the text. The Return Button recalls the screen that was in use when Help was selected.

Bibliography opens a screen of the references that are footnoted throughout the SIMIS text. Arrow buttons, which are located at the bottom of the Bibliography screen, navigate though the Bibliography. The Return Button recalls the screen that was in use when Help was selected.

Copyright © 1996 by Harcourt Brace & Company
All rights reserved.

About Tool Bar opens a screen that lists and describes the navigation tools that are used throughout SIMIS. About Marketing . . . provides information about the origin of SIMIS and the authors. Be sure to "rub" the jar!

Navigation Tools

Introductory Screen

The first screen of each chapter is accessed by highlighting the chapter of choice in the left-hand column of the Table of Contents; then highlighting and double clicking Objectives in the right-hand column of the Table of Contents. Navigation buttons, located on the left-hand margin of the screen, open Chapter Objectives, Captains of Industry, Marketing Highlights and an Introductory Video. Each of these features is discussed in more detail in the following sections.

The central area of the screen contains an introduction to the chapter in text form. Vertical scroll bars on the right-hand margin of the screen access additional text.

Chapter Objectives Button

 A list of learning objectives in each chapter appears in the left-hand margin of the opening screen and alerts a student to the type of material to be presented and learned in the chapter. The objectives are accessed by clicking the Chapter Objectives Button. Click on the Objectives screen to return to the main screen.

Captains of Industry Button

 The Captains of Industry Button appears below the Chapter Objectives Button. Click the button to display a picture of the "Captain" and a profile of his or her professional career. Use the vertical scroll bars to access additional text.

Copyright © 1996 by Harcourt Brace & Company
All rights reserved.

The Captains of Industry are profiles of corporate leaders who have made significant contributions to their companies through the practice of marketing. The profiles of these successful marketing leaders also provide information about the variety of careers that are available in marketing. To return to the main screen, click the Return Button.

Marketing Highlights Button

 The Marketing Highlights Button is located below the Captains of Industry Button. Click the button to open the Marketing Highlight text and use the vertical scroll bars to access additional text.

Marketing Highlights are detailed descriptions of actual marketing practices and the application of marketing principles. Each Marketing Highlight has been chosen to illustrate the principles that are developed later in the chapter texts.

Click the Return Button to return to the main screen.

Video Button

 A Video Button will always appear on the first screen of each chapter and will occasionally appear in the lower left-hand corner of chapter screens when videos are available. Click the button to start the video. When the video has finished playing, the screen that you were viewing will be recalled automatically. The video may be stopped before it has finished by clicking on the video screen itself.

The introductory videos describe companies and their products or introduce corporate executives who discuss marketing strategies. Each video provides a real-life illustration of the marketing principles that are developed throughout the chapter.

It is recommended that students view the video before reading the chapter material and then later return to the video to associate the newly learned material with the video content. Instructors may use the video as a basis for class discussion.

Copyright © 1996 by Harcourt Brace & Company
All rights reserved.

The video is shown in quarter-screen size to provide the clearest resolution possible. The state of technology at the time of SIMIS development is the limiting factor on video screen size.

Between Section Navigation

Chapters are divided into sections represented by screens that contain text and graphics. Each screen contains navigation tools to assist in moving from section to section and returning to the Table of Contents. Between-the-section navigation tools are described below.

SIMIS Tip

The current section number is displayed in the lower right-hand margin of the section screen. If the number is in decimal form, e.g., 4.2, the current screen is a subsection. In this example, 4.2 would represent Subsection 2 of Section 4.

Left Arrow Button

 Click the Left Arrow Button to move one section at a time toward the beginning of the chapter. The Button becomes inactive when the first section of the chapter is reached or when movement between sections is not possible.

Right Arrow Button

 Click the Right Arrow Button to move one section at time toward the end of the chapter. The Button becomes inactive when the last section of the chapter is reached or when movement between sections is not possible.

Copyright © 1996 by Harcourt Brace & Company
All rights reserved.

Gray Arrow Button

 The Gray Arrow Button, either left or right, is an inactive button and indicates that movement in the direction of the button is not possible.

Wheel Button

 The Wheel Button recalls the Table of Contents that is positioned at the beginning of the program. Use this navigation tool first to recall the Table of Contents and then to move among chapters or to select additional sections within the current chapter.

Within Section Navigation

Chapter sections consist of pages of text that can be manipulated by using Within Section Navigation tools. The following descriptions explain the functions of the navigation tools that are found on the chapter-section screens.

Full-Screen Button

 Click the Full-Screen Button, the first button in the lower screen tool bar, to increase the text to full-screen size for easier reading. Double click on the text to return to the main screen and permit additional navigation to occur.

Notepad Button

 The Notepad is included in the SIMIS program to provide a means for taking notes electronically while studying. To access the Notepad click the Notepad Button, the second button in the tool bar. A notepad will open on the right-hand side of the screen replacing the screen's graphic.

Copyright © 1996 by Harcourt Brace & Company
All rights reserved.

Three additional buttons, which appear at the bottom of the Notepad, open an existing Notepad file, save a current Notepad, or copy text to the Notepad.

SIMIS Tip

To open a new Notepad with a new name—to take notes for another chapter—save the contents of the present Notepad and then close the SIMIS program. Reopen the program and open a new Notepad for the next chapter. Save the new Notepad with a different name.

The Notepad has been designed for two types of use—copying text to the Notepad or summarizing text content and typing it in the Notepad. For copying text into the Notepad, highlight the text with the mouse cursor and then click the Notepad Copy Button. When typing material into it, the Notepad is used as a word processor. Click the Notepad Button with a partially drawn window-shade to close the Notepad.

At the end of a study session, use the Notepad Save Button to save the Notepad contents to a floppy disk. Recall the Notepad file for the new study session with the Notepad Open Button.

The contents of a Notepad may be printed by using a word processor. The Notepad contents are saved as ASCII text, which most word processors are able to read. The Notepad contents cannot be printed directly from the SIMIS program.

More Button

 From time to time when a subject requires additional development or explanation, Support Pages are added to a chapter section. When Support Pages are available, a More Button appears as the third button in the tool bar. Click this button to access the Support Pages; click the Return Button to recall the main screen.

Copyright © 1996 by Harcourt Brace & Company
All rights reserved.

Graph Button

 Text material in SIMIS is often illustrated with the use of charts and graphs. When one of these illustrations is available, the Graph Button appears as the fourth button in the tool bar. Click the Graph Button to open the illustration; click the Return Button to close the illustration.

Return Button

 A Return Button appears when navigation has occurred away from a main screen, e.g., Glossary, Bibliography, and Support Pages. Click the Return Button to recall the main screen.

Up Button

 The Up Button, which is located in the top, right-hand margin of the text material, is used to navigate toward the beginning of the text within a section. Click the button to move one page toward the beginning of the text. When movement in that direction is no longer possible, the button becomes inactive and changes to gray.

SIMIS Tip

A page index is located in the lower, right-hand margin of the screen. The index indicates the current page out of total number of pages of text for the current section or subsection. For example, 2/15 indicates that page 2 is the current page and there are 15 pages of text in the section or subsection.

Down Button

 The Down Button, which is located in the lower, right-hand margin of the text material, is used to navigate toward the end of the text within a section. When movement in that direction is no longer possible, the button becomes inactive and changes to gray.

Copyright © 1996 by Harcourt Brace & Company
All rights reserved.

Hot Words

Hot Words, which are red and contrast to the normal font, are located throughout the text. Click a Hot Word to open a box that contains a definition of the word or phrase that is encoded in the red font. Click on the box to close it and return to the screen that was initially on view.

End of Chapter Navigation

Chapter Review Button

 A set of multiple choice review questions are located at the end of each chapter. Click the Chapter Review Button to display the questions.

The Chapter Review Questions are provided as the means to test your comprehension of the chapter material. When a question is answered the program signals whether a correct answer is chosen.. If an incorrect answer is chosen, the correct answer is identified and a Click to Review Button appears. Recall the text from which the question was taken by clicking the Click to Review Button. After reviewing the text click the Return Button Study Q's Button to recall the Chapter Review Questions. Use the Right Arrow Button or the Left Arrow Button to navigate through the review questions.

Discussion Questions

 Four essay style Discussion Questions, which are included at the end of each chapter, are accessed by clicking the Discussion Question button and dismissed by clicking the Return Button. Instructors may use these questions as a basis for class discussion.

Copyright © 1996 by Harcourt Brace & Company
All rights reserved.

Study Suggestions

Individuals generally develop a style for studying that is comfortable and probably unique to them. The following study suggestions are just that–suggestions for the use of the SIMIS features that can be incorporated as a whole or selectively into one's own personal style.

Study Suggestions for SIMIS Users

Class Preparation

When a chapter has been assigned by the instructor, the following steps are recommended for class preparation.

1. Use the printed textbook for the first reading of the chapter material; then use SIMIS for the remaining steps.

2. Carefully read the chapter objectives to gain an understanding of the what the student is expected to learn from this assignment.

3. Watch the chapter's introductory video to relate the chapter material to real-life situations.

4. Read the Captains of Industry to become acquainted with an individual and an industry that is affected by the principles that are developed in the chapter. Note the types of skills that a marketing executive uses as his or her career unfolds.

5. Read the Marketing Highlight to become familiar with the application of the chapter principles in an actual marketing situation.

6. Using SIMIS reread the chapter text and make an outline of the salient points with the electronic notepad. At the end of the chapter, save and print the outline for later review.

7. Use the end of the chapter review questions to assess your comprehension of the chapter material. If a questions is

Copyright © 1996 by Harcourt Brace & Company
All rights reserved.

answered incorrectly, use the automatic text recall feature to review the appropriate text material.

8. Watch the introductory video again and make notes on the chapter principles that are discussed in the video and their implications for developing marketing policy.

9. Return to the end of the chapter and write concise answers to each of the discussion questions.

10. Immediately before class, review the notes that were created in the SIMIS notepad.

11. In the classroom, participate actively in discussions and take notes on the additional material that is provided by the instructor. The instructor may furnish a lecture outline with extra space for notes. If it is available, the outline is an excellent resource to reduce the amount of in-class writing and allow more time to focus on the instructor's lecture.

12. Two exercises are included for each chapter. The exercises provide the student with a practical experience involving the subject material in the chapter. A student may complete the exercises for his or her own benefit or the course instructor may assign an exercise for course credit.

Examination Preparation

Generally an instructor will require two exams during the course, one at mid-course and a final. If the exams are in-class and closed-book, the following steps for preparation are recommended.

For each chapter covered by the exam:

1. Read the chapter summary in the SIMIS Manual

2. Review the notes created with the SIMIS notepad.

3. Review the lecture outlines (if available) and class notes including the Discussion Question responses.

Copyright © 1996 by Harcourt Brace & Company
All rights reserved.

4. Review the end-of-the-chapter review questions.

5. That should do it. Good luck on the exam.

The authors of *Marketing: An Interactive Learning System* and SIMIS hope that the use of this program will provide you with a rewarding and productive learning experience.

Study Suggestions for Book and Manual Users

Class Preparation

When a chapter has been assigned by the instructor, the following steps are recommended for class preparation.

1. Carefully read the chapter objectives in the SIMIS Manual to gain an understanding of the what the student is expected to learn from this assignment.

2. Read the Captains of Industry to become acquainted with an individual and an industry that is affected by the principles that are developed in the chapter. Note the types of skills that a marketing executive uses as his or her career unfolds.

3. Read the Marketing Highlight to become familiar with the application of the chapter principles in an actual marketing situation.

4. Lightly read the assigned chapter in *Marketing: An Interactive Learning System*

5. Reread the chapter outlining the salient points as you read.

6. Use the chapter review questions in the SIMIS Manual to assess your comprehension of the chapter material. The key to the answers is in the manual's Appendix B.

7. Using your notes, write a concise answer for each of the discussion questions in the SIMIS Manual.

8. Immediately before class, review your notes and the answers that you wrote for the discussion questions.

Copyright © 1996 by Harcourt Brace & Company
All rights reserved.

9. In the classroom, participate actively in discussions and take notes on the additional material that is provided by the instructor.

10. Two exercises are included for each chapter. The exercises provide the student with a practical experience involving the subject material in the chapter. A student may complete the exercises for his or her own benefit or the course instructor may assign an exercise for course credit.

Examination Preparation

Generally an instructor will require two exams during the course, one at mid-course and a final. If the exams are in-class and closed-book, the following steps for preparation are recommended.

For each chapter covered by the exam:

1. Read the chapter summary in the SIMIS Manual.

2. Review the notes that you made while reading the chapter.

3. Review the notes from the lecture.

4. Review the answers to the discussion questions and any notes that you took during class discussion of these questions.

5. Review the end-of-the-chapter review questions in the SIMIS Manual.

6. That should do it. Good luck on the exam.

The authors of *Marketing: An Interactive Learning System* hope that the use of this material will provide you with a rewarding and productive learning experience.

Copyright © 1996 by Harcourt Brace & Company
All rights reserved.

Chapter 1

Introduction to Marketing

Learning Objectives

1. Define marketing.

2. Explain the exchange process.

3. List the separations between producers and consumers.

4. Delineate the basic functions of marketing.

5. Describe the four types of utilities and their functions.

6. Contrast the three eras of marketing and describe our society's marketing concept and orientation.

7. Explain the concept of marketing myopia.

8. Understand the concept of non-profit marketing.

9. Identify the elements of the marketing mix.

Chapter Summary

Marketing serves an important function in today's society for all types of businesses both for-profit and not-for-profit. The basis for marketing is exchange whereby two or more parties give something of value to each other to satisfy each party's perceived needs. A service, product, or idea can be exchanged.

Copyright © 1996 by Harcourt Brace & Company
All rights reserved.

Natural separations such as geographical location, lack of information, and timing in production versus demand exist between exchange parties. Marketing is the process that bridges these separations. Several functions such as exchange, logistical, and facilitating functions must be performed by a variety of parties to enable potential exchange parties to complete any exchange.

Marketing creates time, place, and possession utilities for exchange parties. Products are available when and where a consumer wants them thanks to marketing. And services such as credit extension or financing make exchange possible for many parties.

Marketing has not always existed to the degree of sophistication we know today. The practice developed over many decades as companies evolved from focusing their efforts on production to realizing greater sales and profits by focusing efforts on satisfying customer needs. Today, most companies have tried to adopt the marketing concept to some degree. The three fundamental features of the marketing concept are customer orientation, a coordinated effort by all departments to satisfy customers, and achievement of long-run profits through customer satisfaction.

Marketing efforts are not generally directed at an entire population but rather at specific target markets. Marketers develop a coordinated marketing mix consisting of product, pricing, distribution, and promotional strategies to appeal to and convert target consumers into product users. These features can be combined in an unlimited number of ways. The ultimate challenge for the marketer is to develop the appropriate marketing mix that best matches the needs of the target market.

Chapter Exercises

Exercise 1

Copyright © 1996 by Harcourt Brace & Company
All rights reserved.

Consider the multiple exchanges that must take place for a manufacturer of consumer products to place an ad for its products on television or in a magazine. Develop a diagram of the exchanges. The diagram should include the manufacturer, an advertising agency, an advertising medium, the consumer, and others who may be involved. Analyze the exchange process to determine: 1) what is exchanged between each set of two parties, 2) what is the motivation for each exchange to take place, and 3) who are the winners and losers. Write a report of your findings for the instructor or discussion in class.

Exercise 2

Susan Rice is interested in buying a new entertainment center for her television and her roommate's stereo equipment. A number of marketing functions—exchange, logistics, and facilitating—must be performed before she can actually make the purchase. Develop a marketing matrix for this pending purchase. Construct the matrix with the marketing performers (e.g., manufacturer, distributor) on the vertical axis and marketing functions on the horizontal axis. Fill in the squares with the type of marketing services that would normally be performed for each performer/function combination. If you are uncertain about any aspect of your matrix, discuss it with appropriate faculty members or talk to your local television retailer. Prepare your matrix for class discussion or to present to the class instructor.

Chapter Review Questions

(Correct answers are listed in Appendix B.)

1. Marketing is practiced by
   a) only profit-oriented firms.
   b) only public firms.
   c) all organizations to some degree.
   d) only sales firms.

2. An exchange

20

Copyright © 1996 by Harcourt Brace & Company
All rights reserved.

a) needs at least two parties to take place.
b) gives something of value to both parties.
c) satisfies both parties' needs.
d) all of the above.

3. Which of the following is *not* one of the separations that divide buyers and sellers?
a) form utility
b) geography
c) lack of information
d) value

4. Marketing acts to close separations between exchange parties by performing three general categories of functions? Which is *not* one of these categories?
a) exchange functions
b) facilitating functions
c) perceptual functions
d) logistical functions

5. Standardizing and grading represent
a) a facilitating function created by marketing.
b) a form of utility created by marketing.
c) a separation between buyers and sellers.
d) all of the above.

6. Which department in an organization creates form utility?
a) marketing
b) finance
c) production
d) accounting

7. In the evolution of marketing, which era prevailed until around 1930 in the United States?
a) production
b) financial
c) marketing

21
Copyright © 1996 by Harcourt Brace & Company
All rights reserved.

d)   sales

8.   What is *not* one of the three fundamental features of the marketing concept?
        a)   customer focus
        b)   coordinated effort by all departments
        c)   profits through customer satisfaction
        d)   efficiency of production

9.   The organization-wide generation of market intelligence, dissemination of intelligence across departments, and organization-wide responsiveness to it is called
        a)   marketing myopia.
        b)   market orientation.
        c)   ownership utility.
        d)   facilitating function.

10.   Which of the following activities is part of the product strategy component of the marketing mix?
        a)   brand naming
        b)   financing
        c)   storing
        d)   sales promotion

11.   Which of the following is true?
        a)   Form-utility creation is the role of marketing.
        b)   Spatial separations are actualized via advertising.
        c)   Ownership separations are actualized via advertising.
        d)   None of the above is true.

12.   The promotional strategy component of a firm's marketing mix is
        a)   its means of rewarding employees.
        b)   synonymous with advertising.
        c)   its means of creating time utility.
        d)   its means of communicating with customers.

22

Copyright © 1996 by Harcourt Brace & Company
All rights reserved.

13. Which of the following is *not* a component of the marketing mix?
    a)   product decisions
    b)   distribution decisions
    c)   profit decisions
    d)   promotion decisions

14. Which of the following are *not* a facilitating function of marketing?
    a)   standardizing and grading
    b)   risk-taking
    c)   financing
    d)   all of the above

15. Which of the following describes a seller's market?
    a)   demand equals supply
    b)   demand exceeds supply
    c)   demand is less than supply
    d)   none of the above

Discussion Questions

1. Discuss how marketing can be used in different organizations. Include in your discussion profit and not-for-profit organizations.

2. Explain the "something of value" that is exchanged when the Air Force advertises to potential recruits. What does the Air Force receive and what does the potential recruit receive?

3. Firms in the U.S. have evolved from a production era to a sales era and finally to a marketing era. Can this evolution be applied to the way Eastern Europe is presently evolving?

4. Discuss the concept of marketing myopia. Provide examples of various firms that define themselves myopically? and more broadly?

Copyright © 1996 by Harcourt Brace & Company
All rights reserved.

Chapter 2

Marketing and Its Environment

Learning Objectives

1. Discuss the analysis of the external environment.

2. Discuss the affects that objectives and resources can have on the firm

3. Discuss the affects that competitive forces can have on the firm.

4. Discuss the affects that economic conditions can have on the firm.

5. Discuss the affects that technological developments can have on the firm.

6. Discuss the affects that political and legal considerations can have on the firm.

7. Discuss the affects that social forces can have on the firm.

Chapter Summary

Marketers face controllable decisions when determining product, price, promotion, and distribution strategies. These decisions are not, however, unconstrained. Rather, a variety of environmental forces, or relatively uncontrollable factors, have a major impact

Copyright © 1996 by Harcourt Brace & Company
All rights reserved.

on both the determination of and eventual success of marketing strategies.

The first such uncontrollable factor is an organization's own objectives and resources. Objectives must be clear and obtainable. Each department can have its own set of objectives. But the individual objectives must be guided by the firm's overall objectives so that the entire company is working together towards the same goals. A firm's resources must also be taken into account when developing strategies and objectives.

Competitive forces is another uncontrollable factor for the marketer. Competition is more intense today because competition comes from local, regional, national, and international marketers. Marketers are also more sophisticated and consumers are better informed. A firm's competitive environment also affects the types of strategies a firm employs.

A third uncontrollable factor is economic conditions. Factors such as business cycles, inflation, unemployment, and income exert the most influence in the economic environment and, therefore, on marketing strategies.

Technological developments is the most manageable uncontrollable force a marketer faces. Firms must be aware of new technologies in the marketplace and turn these advances into opportunities and a competitive edge.

Political and legal considerations are a fifth uncontrollable force for the marketer. Many laws affect each element of the marketing mix. Marketers must be aware of and conform to all laws affecting their business.

The sixth and most difficult uncontrollable force to predict is social forces. Changes in the social and cultural environment affect customer behavior and therefore sales of products. Social forces important to today's marketers include demographic developments, changing age structure, changing American households, income dynamics, and minority population developments.

Copyright © 1996 by Harcourt Brace & Company
All rights reserved.

Chapter Exercises

Exercise 1

Assume that you are interested in opening a new retail business, such as a computer software store, a specialty restaurant, or a bike shop, in your home town. Choose one. Then list the environmental forces that affect marketing decisions. List three factors for each of the environmental forces that may affect your chosen business. Write a report of your analysis and include the marketing strategies that would take advantage of environmental opportunities and counter environmental threats.

Exercise 2

Access the Federal Trade Commission's home page on the Internet. The address is http://www.ftc.gov/index.html.

1. Write a review of the FTC consumer protection activities. Information about these activities can be found under Organizational Structure and the Bureau of Consumer Protection. Each of these menu items are hypertext words on the FTC homepage. Be prepared to discuss your report in class.

2. Review recent rulings set forth by the FTC and their implications for marketing managers. A listing of recent rulings can be found under News Releases, an item in hypertext located on the FTC homepage. Select the current or most recent month, then choose three news releases about companies that are involved with consumer products. Summarize the news releases and discuss their implications for marketing managers. Be prepared to discuss your report in class.

Chapter Review Questions

(Correct answers are listed in Appendix B.)

1. Which of the following is *not* an uncontrollable factor for the marketer?

26

Copyright © 1996 by Harcourt Brace & Company
All rights reserved.

    a)   competitive forces
    b)   pricing decisions
    c)   economic conditions
    d)   social forces

2.   Environmental scanning
    a)   is the collection of pertinent information about the marketing environment.
    b)   can be obtained from marketing research units.
    c)   can be obtained from government data.
    d)   all of the above are correct.

3.   Company objectives
    a)   are not needed if each department has set its own objectives.
    b)   should be as general as possible so as not to be too restrictive.
    c)   are necessary so the whole company is working towards the same goals.
    d)   should be idealistic.

4.   Which of the following best captures the meaning of "environment" as used in the context of marketing?
    a)   Environment refers to the weather conditions that influence many marketing decisions, such as retail sales on a rainy day.
    b)   Environment refers specifically to competitive activity.
    c)   Environment refers to the various social forces that influence marketing decisions.
    d)   None of the above adequately capture the meaning of environment.

5.   When a firm attempts to influence the external environment in which it operates through the implementation of strategies, it is engaging in
    a)   environmental scanning.

Copyright © 1996 by Harcourt Brace & Company
All rights reserved.

b) environmental management.
c) corporate espionage.
d) data snooping.

6. Which market structure is the most common structure in advanced economies such as the United States?
   a) pure competition
   b) oligopoly
   c) monopoly
   d) monopolistic competition

7. A certain market structure is characterized as one where many firms sell the same basic product, no one competitor has the power to affect supply or price, all buyers and sellers are assumed to have full knowledge of the market. The described market structure is a(n) _____ structure.
   a) pure competitive
   b) oligopolistic
   c) monopolistic competitive
   d) monopolistic

8. A certain market structure is characterized as one where a large number of sellers produce and sell similar products that are differentiated by minor characteristics. Competition is intense, and consumers' images of products are a major determinant of prices. This is a(n) _____ structure.
   a) pure competitive
   b) oligopolistic
   c) monopolistic competitive
   d) monopolistic

9. When organizations work together toward a common goal, such as the collaboration between Ford and Mazda in the case of the Probe GT. this is termed a
   a) cooperative effort.

28

Copyright © 1996 by Harcourt Brace & Company
All rights reserved.

b)   strategic alliance.
c)   dualistic endeavor.
d)   none of the above are correct.

10.   Which is not a business cycle?
a)   market maturity
b)   prosperity
c)   recession
d)   recovery

11.   A household's after-tax income is called
a)   disposable income.
b)   discretionary income.
c)   nondiscretionary income.
d)   indisposable income.

12.   A household's income that remains after the basic
necessities are purchased is called
a)   disposable income.
b)   discretionary income.
c)   nondiscretionary income.
d)   indisposable income.

13.   The so-called Consumer Bill of Rights includes all of the
following except
a)   the right to safety.
b)   the right to be informed
c)   the right to choose
d)   the right to be satisfied

14.   Which of the following is *not* a procompetitive law?
a)   The Sherman Antitrust Act
b)   The Clayton Act
c)   The Consumer Product Safety Act
d)   The Robinson-Patman Act

Copyright © 1996 by Harcourt Brace & Company
All rights reserved.

15. The act that is explicitly designed to prevent price discrimination is the
    a) Robinson-Patman Act.
    b) Sherman Antitrust Act.
    c) Wheeler-Lea Act.
    d) Federal Trade Commission Act.

16. The Robinson-Patman Act deals with price discrimination for all transactions except between
    a) manufacturers and retailers.
    b) manufacturers and wholesalers.
    c) wholesalers and retailers.
    d) retailers and consumers.

17. Under the Robinson-Patman Act, a manufacturer is justified in charging nonequivalent prices to different customers except in the following situations?
    a) When the price differential can be justified in terms of cost savings to the manufacturer.
    b) When competition forces a manufacturer to charge a lower price to one of its customers than to another.
    c) When it is the manufacturer's best interest to charge different prices to different customers, because doing so is more profitable.
    d) All of the above are justifiable instances for charging nonequivalent prices.

18. Which of the following acts expanded the powers of the Federal Trade Commission to prohibit practices that might injure the public without necessarily affecting competition?
    a) Clayton Act
    b) Robinson-Patman Act
    c) Truth in Advertising Act
    d) Wheeler-Lea Act

Copyright © 1996 by Harcourt Brace & Company
All rights reserved.

19. The National Advertising Review Board is
    a) under the jurisdiction of the Federal Trade Commission.
    b) should be as general as possible so as not to be too restrictive.
    c) the most recent federal agency.
    d) a self-regulatory body.

20. During the 1990s the U.S. population is expected to increase by approximately _____ percent.
    a) 1
    b) 3
    c) 7
    d) 20

21. By the year 2000, the median age of the U.S. population is expected to be
    a) 23 years.
    b) 28 years.
    c) 36 years.
    d) 44 years.

22. Baby boomers were born between the years 1946 and
    a) 1952.
    b) 1958.
    c) 1964.
    d) 1977.

23. By the year 2000, African Americans will account for approximately _____ percent of the U.S. population.
    a) 5
    b) 13
    c) 20
    d) 25

24. Which ethnic group in the U.S. is the best educated and highest income earning?

31

Copyright © 1996 by Harcourt Brace & Company
All rights reserved.

a) African Americans
b) White Americans
c) Hispanic Americans
d) Asian Americans

25. Which of the following is *not* an accurate statement about Generation X Americans?
   a) They are aged 18-29 years.
   b) They are socially liberal but politically and economically conservative.
   c) They represent a single market by virtue of their homogeneity in buying preferences.
   d) All of the above are equally correct.

Discussion Questions

1. Merck has been the premier drug manufacturer for decades. Environmental changes, however, have caused Merck's management to reassess the way they are doing business, particularly their distribution of drugs. What type of environmental scanning do you feel is especially important for a drug manufacturer in today's environment?

2. The management of Bell South feels that future growth potential for the company is in high-quality, interactive communication. The technology to deliver this type of communication is likely to be in fiber-optic cables, but Federal Regulations prevent Bell South from engaging in the cable business in its territory. What type of environmental scanning should the management of Bell South undertake to prepare for the future?

3. The sales of heavy equipment manufacturers like Clark Equipment and Caterpillar are strongly affected by the economic environment. What stage of the business cycle would you say they are currently experiencing? What would you recommend to a heavy equipment manufacturer regarding the economic effects on sales?

32

Copyright © 1996 by Harcourt Brace & Company
All rights reserved.

4. Bicycle sales have flourished in the past because of interest in cycling for exercise and health reasons. What social trends do you see occurring at the present time that may affect bicycle sales positively or negatively over the next five years?

Copyright © 1996 by Harcourt Brace & Company
All rights reserved.

Chapter 3

Role of Research in Marketing

Learning Objectives

1. Define marketing research.

2. Discuss marketing information and decision support systems.

3. Explain the steps of market research.

4. Describe who does market research.

5. Define the two types of research data.

6. Describe the types of research firms.

7. Explain the process of market research.

8. Discuss the methods of primary research.

9. List the advantages and disadvantages of primary and secondary research.

Chapter Summary

A well-designed research study can provide the answers to almost any marketing dilemma. Marketing decision makers need good, reliable information as the basis for marketing strategies. Internal information, information that comes from within the company itself, typically is in the form of company reports. External data is information that has been generated from outside

Copyright © 1996 by Harcourt Brace & Company
All rights reserved.

the company. All of this information must be collected, organized, and made available in a usable form for management. Today, companies use marketing information systems and decision support systems to gather data from internal and external sources, synthesize the information, and disseminate it to decision makers.

Syndicated service firms specialize in providing secondary data, or previously published data to organizations. Full-service research firms specialize in providing primary data, or information collected specifically for a purpose. The marketing research process includes problem definition, research design and data collection (via observation, survey, or experimental methods), and analysis, interpretation, and presentation of findings. A researcher must keep in mind the company's needs and the study's objectives, analyze the data accordingly, and present the findings in a clear, understandable manner.

Chapter Exercises

Exercise 1

Assume that you have been hired to assess the location and effectiveness of point-of-purchase displays in a clothing store. In a local shopping mall choose a store where you can unobstrusively observe the traffic pattern.

Identify one or two prominent point-of-purchase displays. Observe the shopping behavior of five customers, one at a time. Note the customers' shopping patterns, whether they pay attention to the displays, whether the display influences their shopping behavior, and the amount of time spent in the store. Write a report of your findings and recommendations to hand in or present to the class.

You may wish to discuss your project with the store manager to obtain his or her permission to conduct the observations. The store manager may also be willing to discuss how the company

Copyright © 1996 by Harcourt Brace & Company
All rights reserved.

uses store displays and, after you have completed your observations, comment on your findings.

Exercise 2

Market research companies often conduct exploratory research on consumer products to identify problems or successes that consumers have when using the product.

To simulate this research, choose a consumer product that is used widely by fellow students. Construct 3 or 4 open ended questions that will collect data about when the product is used, how it is used on each usage occasion, and what the user likes or dislikes about the product for each usage occasion.

Using your questions, interview five or six fellow students to collect data about the product. Write a report of your findings; include recommendations for marketing strategies.

Chapter Review Questions

(Correct answers are listed in Appendix B.)

1.   Which of the following is the best description of a marketing information system (MIS)?
    a)   A MIS is just another name for a marketing research study such as a telephone survey.
    b)   A MIS is the name given to information about a company's competitors.
    c)   A MIS is a company's marketing-relevant database consisting of internal and external data.
    d)   A MIS is just another name for a company's management information system.

2.   _____ data is information collected by or for an organization to address that organization's specific research question or needs.
    a)   Primary

Copyright © 1996 by Harcourt Brace & Company
All rights reserved.

b)   Secondary
c)   Marketing research
d)   Marketing information system

3.   The collection of data to gain a greater understanding of the research question is termed
a)   secondary data collection.
b)   primary data collection.
c)   syndicated research.
d)   exploratory research.

4.   Which of the following marketing research techniques would be least acceptable if the research purpose were to determine buying motives that underlie consumers' product choices?
a)   survey research
b)   experimental research
c)   observation research
d)   all of these are equally acceptable

5.   Which of the following survey techniques can generally be expected to yield the highest response rate?
a)   Telephone interviews
b)   Mail questionnaires
c)   Personal interviews
d)   There are no notable differences among these techniques with respect to response rates.

6.   A specialized form of interviewing where a moderator leads a small informal group discussion is called a
a)   miniature interview.
b)   focus group.
c)   syndication group.
d)   None of the above.

7.   Which of the following is *not* an advantage of primary data collection?

Copyright © 1996 by Harcourt Brace & Company
All rights reserved.

a) The data are current.
b) The data fit the specific purpose of the marketing issue at hand.
c) The marketer has complete control over the research methodology.
d) The data are assured of being representative of the population and completely valid.

8. Compared to primary data, which of the following is *not* an advantage of secondary data?
   a) Secondary data are less expensive.
   b) Secondary data are available more quickly.
   c) Secondary data better fit the researcher's exact needs.
   d) All of these are relative advantages of secondary data.

9. Another term for "population" as it relates to the sampling aspect of data collection is
   a) sampling frame.
   b) strata.
   c) cluster.
   d) None of these terms are interchangeable with population.

10. A researcher has a complete list of all the students who are advertising majors at a certain university. One hundred of these students are randomly sampled by selecting numbers from a random number table. The researcher has employed which sampling method to select these 100 names?
    a) cluster sampling
    b) stratified sampling
    c) purposive sampling
    d) simple random sampling

Copyright © 1996 by Harcourt Brace & Company
All rights reserved.

11. A researcher has a complete list of all the city blocks in a certain town. The researcher randomly samples three blocks and then interviews every homeowner who resides in each of the three blocks. Which sampling methods has the researcher used?
   a) cluster sampling
   b) stratified sampling
   c) purposive sampling
   d) simple random sampling

12. A researcher is interested in determining the average salary of major league baseball players. To save time, the researcher decides to select a sample of 60 ball players. Rather than taking a random sample of all players, he decides to delineate the players into three groups of positions–infielders, outfielders, and pitchers–and to take separate random samples of 20 players from each category. What sampling procedure has the researcher used?
   a) cluster sampling
   b) stratified sampling
   c) purposive sampling
   d) simple random sampling

13. A student is conducting a little study to determine how many soft drinks students in her dorm consume on average each day. She stops the first 24 students she sees and asks them to indicate how many soft drinks they consume per day on average. Her sampling method is
   a) simple random sampling.
   b) complex random sampling.
   c) unpurposive sampling.
   d) convenience sampling.

Copyright © 1996 by Harcourt Brace & Company
All rights reserved.

Discussion Questions

1. The owner of a privately owned women's clothing store is concerned about losing sales to a new national chain store that has recently opened in her city. To improve her marketing ability, she is considering a basic marketing decision support system. What type of data would you suggest that she gather and how should she gather it?

2. You are interested in opening a computer software store in the vicinity of your University, but you are uncertain whether sufficient demand exists to support the store. What research steps should be taken to determine the level of demand?

3. Procter and Gamble's product manager for Downy wants the most up-to-date information about his product's performance. What type of data would you recommend that he gather and from which source?

4. When making the decision to gather data, the researcher generally has both primary and secondary data available. What are the advantages and disadvantages of gathering either type of data?

Copyright © 1996 by Harcourt Brace & Company
All rights reserved.

Chapter 4

Consumer Behavior

Learning Objectives

1. Describe how the environmental factors influence consumer behavior.

2. Describe how the internal factors influence consumer behavior.

Chapter Summary

A successful marketer must have a good understanding of why customers buy or don't buy their products. This is a difficult task since consumer behavior is complex, dynamic, and unpredictable. Many influences directly affect consumer buying behavior.

Environmental influences that influence consumer behavior include culture (consumer's set of values), social class (group sharing economic status and similar consumer behavior), personal influences (a consumer's reference group), family (group related by blood or marriage sharing a household), and situational influences (factors specific to a particular buying choice). One or several of these factors can act together in determining a consumer's buying decision.

Individual differences and psychological processes, factors that are internal to the consumer, also affect consumer behavior. These factors include motivation and involvement; learning,

41

Copyright ©1996 by Harcourt Brace & Company
All rights reserved.

information processing, knowledge and attitudes; and personality and psychographics. Understanding consumer needs, or motives, is a basic premise of marketing. Marketers must identify what needs their products satisfy and create an effective marketing mix to convince the consumer of their products' value.

A consumer's decision process is the third factor that affects consumer behavior. A typical decision process includes the recognition of a need, the search for information, an evaluation of alternatives, a purchase decision, and a postpurchase evaluation. The time and depth devoted to a decision process varies by situation and consumer. Decision processes can be classified in the following categories based on the complexity of the decision: routinized response behavior (requires little time and energy), limited problem solving (moderate amount of time and search), or extended problem solving (lengthy process with considerable external search).

Chapter Exercises

Exercise 1

Go to a local popular restaurant for a late-night snack. Observe approximately six patrons and write a description of their clothing styles. Identify, if possible, the environmental influences that led to the choice of wardrobe for each of your subjects. Write a report from your findings and include marketing suggestions for local clothing retailers.

Exercise 2

Choose a product category that is popular among your friends, (e.g., face and body lotions, computers, or local restaurants). Interview 5 or 6 friends who use the chosen product category to determine the product attributes that are important to them when choosing a particular brand. Then, ask *why* those attributes are important. Write a report that describes how attitudes are formed toward brands of your chosen product category.

Copyright ©1996 by Harcourt Brace & Company
All rights reserved.

Chapter Review Questions

(Correct answers are listed in Appendix B.)

1. Which of the following is *not* an external force, or environmental influence, on individual consumer behavior?
    a)   Culture.
    b)   Social class.
    c)   Psychographics.
    d)   All of the above are environmental influences.

2. Which of the following statements best captures the essence of culture's influence on consumer behavior?
    a)   Cultural values, when internalized, influence individual actions, including consumer behavior.
    b)   Cultured individuals have higher social class, which is the means by which culture influences consumer behavior.
    c)   Cultural values create knowledge structures, or schemas, that guide an individual's consumer behavior.
    d)   All of the above are equally correct.

3. Social class
    a)   no longer exists in the United States.
    b)   is the term sociologists use to refer to one's occupation.
    c)   is a group of individuals who share similar economic status.
    d)   is unaffected by one's occupation.

4. The single best determinant of social class status is one's
    a)   personal wealth.
    b)   occupation.
    c)   level of education.
    d)   where one lives.

Copyright ©1996 by Harcourt Brace & Company
All rights reserved.

5. The "capitalist class" in Gilbert and Kahl's framework for delineating social classes represents approximately ___% of the American population?
    a) 1
    b) 5
    c) 10
    d) 25

6. Pedro Cuello is an upper manager in a large American corporation. His family income runs nearly twice the national average. According to the Gilbert and Kahl social class system, Pedro would be classified as falling in the
    a) capitalist class.
    b) upper middle class.
    c) middle middle class.
    d) middle class.

7. A reference group
    a) dictates how its members should act.
    b) can be an individual or a group.
    c) has a powerful influence on its members.
    d) all of the above.

8. A consumer is most likely to accept and respond to word-of-mouth influences when
    a) the consumer lacks sufficient information to make an informed choice.
    b) the product is easy to evaluate using objective criteria.
    c) the decision process involved is simple.
    d) it comes from a salesperson.

9. In terms of buying decisions, who is the main decision maker in a family?
    a) father

44

Copyright ©1996 by Harcourt Brace & Company
All rights reserved.

b) mother

c) different family members depending on the purchase

d) the user

10. In the decision-making process, the person who initiates thinking about buying products and the gathering of information to aid the decision is the

a) influencer.

b) gatekeeper.

c) decider.

d) buyer.

11. Which of the following is *not* a situational influence that affects consumer behavior?

a) physical surroundings

b) social surroundings

c) time

d) cultural values

12. In the decision-making process, the person whose opinions are sought concerning criteria the family should use in purchases and which products or brands most likely fit those evaluative criteria is termed a(n)

a) influencer.

b) gatekeeper.

c) decider.

d) buyer.

13. Associative learning occurs when

a) a consumer follows his reference group's advice.

b) a consumer forms hypotheses about consumption alternatives.

c) a consumer draws connections between environmental events.

d) a consumer integrates new information with pre-existing beliefs.

45

Copyright ©1996 by Harcourt Brace & Company
All rights reserved.

14. Retention is the information processing stage when
    a) a consumer agrees with a marketing message.
    b) marketplace information is taken into long-term memory.
    c) relevant marketplace information reaches one or more of the five senses.
    d) marketing stimuli are interpreted.

15. Once an attitude is developed
    a) it becomes effective.
    b) it becomes cognitive
    c) it can easily be changed.
    d) it is relatively enduring.

16. Which of the following sequences best represents the stages of information processing?
    a) attention, comprehension, exposure, acceptance, retention
    b) comprehension, exposure, attention, acceptance, retention
    c) acceptance, comprehension, exposure, attention, retention
    d) exposure, attention, comprehension, acceptance, retention

17. Cognitive response activity such as counter argumentation occurs at which information processing stage?
    a) exposure
    b) retention
    c) acceptance
    d) attention

18. Three of the following terms represent related concepts. Which of the terms does not belong?
    a) associative network

46

Copyright ©1996 by Harcourt Brace & Company
All rights reserved.

b) knowledge structure
c) comprehension
d) schema

19. Given an expensive, infrequently purchased product, the attitude formation process is best characterized according to which of the following sequences of attitude components?
a) conative→cognitive→affective
b) conative→affective→cognitive
c) cognitive→conative→affective
d) cognitive→affective→conative

20. Given an inexpensive, frequently purchased product, the attitude formation process is best characterized according to which of the following sequences of attitude components?
a) conative→cognitive→affective
b) conative→affective→cognitive
c) cognitive→conative→affective
d) cognitive→affective→conative

21. Which of the following attitude change strategies is most frequently used?
a) Changing an existing belief on which the attitude is based.
b) Changing the perceived importance of a product attribute.
c) Encouraging consumers to consider a different attribute or product benefit that has not been considered before.
d) All of these are used with equal frequency.

22. Using the language of classical conditioning, an advertised brand is equivalent to a(n)
a) unconditioned response (UR).

47

Copyright ©1996 by Harcourt Brace & Company
All rights reserved.

b)   conditioned response (CR).

c)   conditioned stimulus (CS).

d)   unconditioned stimulus (US).

23.   The brands that a consumer devotes serious thoughts to buying constitute his or her

a)   consideration set.

b)   evaluative criteria.

c)   schema.

d)   psychographic profile.

Discussion Questions

1. How would a consumer's decision buying process differ when purchasing a new personal computer or when purchasing a gallon of milk?

2. How do the product characteristics vary to cause the different decision processes in Question 1?

3. How can a marketer modify consumer attitudes held toward his or her product?

4. What roles are various members of a family likely to play when choosing a family vacation?

Copyright ©1996 by Harcourt Brace & Company
All rights reserved.

Chapter 5

Organizational Buying Behavior

Learning Objectives

1. Distinguish between customers and consumers.

2. Describe the four major types of customers who utilize organizational marketing.

3. Discuss three distinguishing characteristics of organizational marketing.

4. Describe the types of organizational buying decisions.

5. Explain the basic organizational buying process.

6. Define and explain the value of SIC codes.

Chapter Summary

Organizational marketing is the marketing of products and services to organizations, both business and nonbusiness, rather than consumers. There are four types of organizational customers: Producers are individuals and organizations that purchase goods and services used in the production of other products for the purpose of making a profit. Resellers are intermediaries such as wholesalers, brokers/agents, and retailers who buy finished products to resell for a profit. The government sector is comprised of the federal, state, and local governmental units. Finally, nonbusiness institutions are organizations that provide services without the motivation of profit.

49

Copyright © 1996 by Harcourt Brace & Company
All rights reserved.

Organizational buying behavior is similar to consumer buying behavior in that price, quality, service, and dependability are all considered important factors to varying degrees. However, differences exist between the two markets also. Most industries are geographically concentrated with a limited number of customers. Demand in the organizational market also differs from consumer demand in that it is derived (dependent on the demand of consumer goods), inelastic (not significantly affected by short-term changes in price), joint (two or more products are used in the production of one product), and fluctuating (more unsteady). In the organizational market, multiple parties are involved in the process more so than in the consumer market. Often buying centers are called upon to make major purchases for the organization.

Not all organizational buying decisions are the same. The straight rebuy, which requires little time and effort, is a purchase that can be handled on a purely routine basis. In a modified rebuy, the purchaser requires some additional information or a minor change to the original product. A new buy is the purchase of a product or service for the first time. Each situation requires different amounts of time, research, and negotiations.

Organizational customers are classified by their area of specialization, size, location, and goods purchased. The Standard Industrial Classification System (SIC) as developed by the federal government provides information on organizational customers. This information is valuable to organizational marketers in identifying prospective customers.

Chapter Exercises

Exercise 1

Select from the library a trade magazine, such as *Restaurant,* and thumb through it noticing the ads. Choose four or five ads that are outstanding in some way and write a brief description of each ad. Analyze the approach that is used in the ads, noting particularly which members of the buying center the ads address.

Copyright © 1996 by Harcourt Brace & Company
All rights reserved.

Write a report of your findings to give to the class instructor or discuss in class.

Exercise 2

Apple's Macintosh computer is sold in a variety of markets including consumer, government, and business. Select magazines that are likely to address each of these markets and are likely to include ads for computers, preferably Macintosh. Search for ads in each of the market categories and photocopy examples from each category. Write an analysis of the differences and similarities that are used by advertisers when approaching the different markets.

Chapter Review Questions

(Correct answers are listed in Appendix B.)

1. How do business-to-business markets differ from consumer markets?
   a) They sell more products.
   b) Consumer demand is derived from organizational demand
   c) They tend to be more geographically concentrated.
   d) Organizational markets have more customers.

2. Joint demand occurs when
   a) increases or decreases in product prices do not significantly affect demand.
   b) demand fluctuates.
   c) the level of demand for organizational products is dependent on the demand for consumer products.
   d) two or more products are used in the production of a final product.

3. Which of the following explanations best explains why the demand for business-to-business products is relatively inelastic?

51

Copyright © 1996 by Harcourt Brace & Company
All rights reserved.

a)	The price for one component in a finished product is only a fraction of the total price of the final product for which it is a part.
b)	A decline in the availability of one product causes a decline in the production of the final product.
c)	A small change in consumer demand results in a large change in manufacturing operations.
d)	These products are rarely advertised.

4.	A buying center
a)	is a group of key employees with different expertise joined together to make major purchases.
b)	is made up of a group of purchasing agents who have different backgrounds and experience; however, all are employed in the purchasing department.
c)	must have a minimum of five members.
	is used for all company purchases.

5.	The primary determinant of who the "decide" is in the decision process is
a)	the budget.
b)	the individual who has the most information regarding the purchase,
c)	the size and importance of the purchase.
d)	the level of need for the product.

6.	Which type of organizational purchase requires complete negotiations?
a)	straight rebuy
b)	new task
c)	modified rebuy
d)	buying center purchases

7.	The concept of a buying stream is based on the premise that

52

Copyright © 1996 by Harcourt Brace & Company
All rights reserved.

a) all industrial buying stems from the need to solve a problem.
b) all companies need to buy products for business use.
c) all purchases must go through a buying process within the company.
d) technical problem solvers are needed to investigate and solve problems.

8. SIC codes are
   a) government codes covering buying procedures.
   b) a detailed system that classifies companies according to their lines of business.
   c) codes for classifying manufacturers of industrial products.
   d) codes for planning organizational activities.

9. Which of the following is *not* a characteristic of organizational markets?
   a) derived demand
   b) inelastic demand
   c) elastic demand
   d) joint demand

10. Which of the following best captures the concept of derived demand?
   a) The demand for cereal is influenced by the supply for wheat and other grains.
   b) The demand for wheat is dependent on the supply of competitive foodstuffs (rice, corn, etc.)
   c) The demand for cereal depends on the demand for good-eating habits among consumers and the availability of other breakfast foods.
   d) The demand for wheat, corn, and rice is determined in part by the demand for cereal.

Copyright © 1996 by Harcourt Brace & Company
All rights reserved.

11. Product X is made of components A and B. The availability of component B has dramatically declined; hence the demand for component A is substantially reduced. This description characterizes which form of demand condition?
a) fluctuating
b) derived
c) elastic
d) joint

12. Product X is made of components A, B, C, D, and E. The price of component D increases, but the manufacturer of Product X does not reduce its demand for this component. This description characterizes which form of demand condition?
a) fluctuating
b) derived
c) inelastic
d) joint

13. In organizational buying, the individuals who control the flow of information regarding a purchase are termed
a) gatekeepers.
b) influencers.
c) peacemakers.
d) none of the above.

14. A manufacturer of lawn products (lawnmowers, riding mowers, etc.) has spent months investigating the best possible supplier from which to purchase tires. Individuals from production, engineering, purchasing, and the finance department were involved in the decision. These individuals constituted a
a) purchase squad.
b) buying center.
c) purchasing task force.
d) buying conglomerate.

54

Copyright © 1996 by Harcourt Brace & Company
All rights reserved.

15. A manufacturer of lawn products (lawnmowers, riding mowers, etc.) has spent months investigating potential suppliers from which to purchase special batteries so that the lawn products manufacturer can convert from gas engines to battery-powered electrical engines. This purchasing decision in this case would be classified as a
   a) new task.
   b) modified rebuy.
   c) straight rebuy.
   d) crucial rebuy.

Discussion Questions

1. Why are industrial markets considered to be more rational than consumer markets.

2. What are the primary concerns of industrial buyers in each of the three types of buying situations?

3. Apple sells computers to both consumers and industrial buyers such as government agencies and educational institutions. What are some of the differences in marketing strategies that Apple may use in the two markets?

4. Monroe Solutions, Inc. sells complete inventory control systems. How could Monroe's marketing manager use SIC codes to develop her marketing plan?

Copyright © 1996 by Harcourt Brace & Company
All rights reserved.

Chapter 6

Market Segmentation

Learning Objectives

1. Explain what is meant by a market.

2. Define the two basic strategies used to identify potential customers.

3. State the criteria for effective segmentation.

4. Explain each of the five bases for segmenting consumer markets.

5. Describe the three bases for segmenting industrial markets.

6. Discuss the steps in planning and implementing a segmentation strategy.

7. Describe the process of developing the marketing mix.

Chapter Summary

A market is a group of customers who have the need or desire, the ability, and the authority to purchase a specific product. Different markets are classified based on who purchases a product and how the product will be used. A product purchased by a consumer for his own use is a consumer product whereas a

Copyright © 1996 by Harcourt Brace & Company
All rights reserved.

product purchased by an organization for use in its business operations is a business-to-business product.

Firms focus their marketing efforts for products on target markets, or groups of consumers with similar needs, rather than on the entire market. These consumers are the most likely to purchase a firm's products.

In developing a strategy to identify its potential customers, marketers may choose to segment or not segment a market. A mass-market strategy is used by a marketer who chooses not to segment—the same product and other marketing mix elements are offered to all customers throughout the market. A market segmentation strategy is used by a marketer who realizes that different groups within the market have different needs and divides the market as such. Firms that concentrate their efforts on a smaller segment of the market use a concentrated market strategy. Firms that target multiple segments with different strategies for each segment use a differentiated market strategy. A firm must target only those segments that its resources realistically permit it to pursue.

Markets can be segmented based on identifiable characteristics of individuals or groups. The five most commonly used categories of segmentation bases include geographic, demographic, psychographic, benefits, and usage characteristics. Business-to-business markets also use segmentation strategies to identify customer groups. These include geographic, customer-based, and end-use application segmentations.

For a segmentation strategy to be successful, the chosen segment must be identifiable and measurable, profitable, economically accessible, and exhibit a relatively homogeneous response function to the marketing mix that is designed for it.

Chapter Exercises

Exercise 1

Copyright © 1996 by Harcourt Brace & Company
All rights reserved.

Purchase three women's magazines to assist in analyzing how marketers position their products for different market segments. The magazines must be clearly oriented toward different female segments, (e.g., teenage, mature, black, Hispanic, Asian). Search through the magazines and clip ads for face and body lotions separating the ads by their magazine source. Analyze the benefits emphasized in the ads and write a report on the positioning strategies that are used by the advertisers.

Exercise 2

Go to a local shoe store or department store shoe section and write a descriptive list of the various styles of shoes for either men or women. (You may wish to narrow your research to either sport shoes or dress and casual shoes to keep the project within reasonable limits.) Analyze your list and write a report on the market segmentation strategies that are used by shoe manufacturers. Include in your report a list of the important segmentation variables.

Chapter Review Questions

(Correct answers are listed in Appendix B.)

1.   What is a market?
   a)   A group of consumers who have similar needs or desires.
   b)   A group of consumers with purchasing ability.
   c)   A group of consumers with purchasing authority.
   d)   All of the above.

2.   What are the advantages of undifferentiated marketing?
   a)   Production costs will be minimized.
   b)   Lower, competitive prices can be offered to consumers.
   c)   A specific image can be built and maintained with consumers.
   d)   All of the above.

Copyright © 1996 by Harcourt Brace & Company
All rights reserved.

3.   Why do organizations implement a market segmentation strategy?
     a)   to deal with the variability in demand
     b)   to achieve lower production costs and retail prices
     c)   to standardize operations
     d)   to appeal to a wide range of consumers within a market

4.   When an organization concentrates its marketing efforts on a smaller segment of a larger market, it is using
     a)   an undifferentiated marketing strategy.
     b)   a differentiated marketing strategy.
     c)   a concentrated marketing strategy.
     d)   a mass market strategy.

5.   Which of the following is *not* a criterion for successful segmentation?
     a)   The segmentation variable must be identifiable and measurable.
     b)   The potential segment must break even.
     c)   The segment must be reachable.
     d)   The segment must show a positive response to the marketing mix.

6.   Which of the following is *not* a potential basis for segmenting markets?
     a)   age
     b)   geographic locale
     c)   lifestyle
     d)   economic accessibility

7.   A Primary Metropolitan Statistical Area (PMSA) is
     a)   a city.
     b)   an area with a population of over 50,000.
     c)   a large urbanized county or cluster of counties with a population of 1 million or more.
     d)   a metropolitan area that includes at least 2 MSAs.

Copyright © 1996 by Harcourt Brace & Company
All rights reserved.

8.	According to VALS 2, which group of consumers are status-oriented?
	a)	experiencers
	b)	achievers
	c)	fulfilleds
	d)	believers

9.	Industrial markets can be segmented based on all except
	a)	geographic location.
	b)	product specifications.
	c)	psychographic characteristics.
	d)	end-use application.

10.	Which of the following VALS 2 groups is considered principle-oriented?
	a)	achievers
	b)	strivers
	c)	believers
	d)	makers

11.	A certain company was considering segmenting its market by directing its efforts at senior citizens. Its marketing research revealed, however, that all senior citizens were not equally responsive to the marketing mix designed for them. In this particular case, age as a potential segmentation variable fails to satisfy which of the following criteria?
	a)	homogeneous response
	b)	measurability
	c)	identifiability
	d)	all of these criteria

12.	The two approaches to a market segmentation strategy are
	a)	concentrated segmentation strategy and undifferentiated segmentation strategy.

Copyright © 1996 by Harcourt Brace & Company
All rights reserved.

b) differentiated segmentation strategy and concentrated segmentation strategy.
c) differentiated segmentation strategy and marketing mix segmentation strategy.
d) none of the above.

13. Which of the following is *not* an advantage of a concentrated segmentation strategy?
a) ease of competition by larger firms
b) allows firm to gain expertise
c) potential cost savings
d) all of the above

14. Which of the following is an example of demographic segmentation?
a) age
b) income
c) education
d) all of the above

15. What does the acronym AIO stand for?
a) Age, Interests, and Occupations
b) Activities, Interests, and Occupations
c) Activities, Interests, and Opinions
d) Age, Income, and Occupations

Discussion Questions

1. Discuss how the following products would be classified first as a consumer product, then how would each become a business-to-business product. Identify potential ways the products would be marketed differently as a consumer product or a business-to-business product: a) personal computer, b) a quart of oil, and c) a pencil.

2. Discuss the basic differences between a concentrated segmentation strategy and a differentiated segmentation

Copyright © 1996 by Harcourt Brace & Company
All rights reserved.

strategy. Choose any company's product and discuss how they could implement each strategy.

3. Develop arguments for why you feel the cereal industry is over-segmented. Develop an argument for why the same industry needs more segmented products.

4. Discuss the five steps in the planning process for implementing a segmentation strategy.

Copyright © 1996 by Harcourt Brace & Company
All rights reserved.

Chapter 7

Planning and Forecasting

Learning Objectives

1. Explain the five key elements of planning.

2. Describe the levels of organizational planning.

3. Discuss the four fundamental elements of strategic planning.

4. Describe BCG's Product Portfolio-Analysis Model.

5. Describe GE's Attractiveness-Business Position Model.

6. Discuss the characteristics of a marketing plan.

7. Understand the components of a marketing plan.

8. Describe the forecasting process.

9. State five popular forecasting methods.

Chapter Summary

Planning is the basis for sound decision making in any situation in life. Strategic planning and forecasting are key activities that influence and direct the development of specific marketing strategies.

The most important level of planning is **strategic planning**, or the organization's overall game plan. This plan typically

63

Copyright © 1996 by Harcourt Brace & Company
All rights reserved.

encompasses the firm's long-range goals and dictates direction for all departments in the firm. Strategic planning differs from marketing planning, or the game plan for a particular product or product line. The marketing plan is the detailed scheme of the marketing strategies and activities associated with each product's marketing mix—product, pricing, distribution, and promotional decisions. **Tactical planning** is another level of organizational planning which involves specifying details that pertain to the organization's activities during the current period.

Strategic planning is comprised of four fundamental elements: organization missions (how an organization defines its business, or what makes it different from competition), strategic business units (smaller divisions, to facilitate planning and general operations), objectives (clear, realistic goals based on measurable achievements such as sales or market share), and strategic planning tools (tools to help managers in their strategic and marketing planning efforts).

Marketing plans emanate from and are inspired by the overall strategic plan. Marketing plans vary in length and formality. A marketing plan can cover a specific product or an entire product line or category. A typical marketing plan includes an executive summary, an analysis of the marketing situation, an assessment of opportunities and threats, specification of marketing objectives, a formulation of marketing strategies, the preparation of action programs and budgets, and the development of control procedures.

A critical element in marketing planning is sales forecasting. Sales forecasts are developed either for the total market or by market segments. In both cases, the market must be able to generate sufficient sales to support the planned marketing activities. Several methods are available that vary in development time and complexity. The method chosen depends on the products being forecast. Some popular methods of forecasting include executive opinion, composite of sales force

Copyright © 1996 by Harcourt Brace & Company
All rights reserved.

estimates, buyer intention surveys, exponential smoothing, and multiple-factor index method.

Chapter Exercises

Exercise 1

Visit an automobile dealer's showroom or the homepage on the Internet for a particular automobile brand, (e.g., Chevrolet, Ford, Toyota, or Nissan). Make a list of the types of automobiles that are produced by the manufacturer, (e.g., Altima, Maxima, Pathfinder, 300Z). Do not include models within types, such as 4-doors vs. 2-doors, convertibles vs. hardtops.

Obtain data from the library or other sources to estimate market share and category growth rate for each of the automobile types. (Estimate unavailable data.) Using these automobile types develop a chart that resembles BCG's Product-Portfolio Matrix and write marketing strategy recommendations for each of the automobile types.

Exercise 2

Choose a small to medium-size business in your local community that you patronize on a regular basis. Make two lists; one list of opportunities that are available or likely to become available for this company; and the other, a list of threats that this company faces now or in the near future. Based on your lists, write recommendations for marketing strategies that will help the company build market strength for the future.

Chapter Review Questions

(Correct answers are listed in Appendix B.)

1. Strategic planning is
    a) a game plan for a particular product.
    b) a plan specifying details for, say, the next three months.
    c) a company's overall game plan.

Copyright © 1996 by Harcourt Brace & Company
All rights reserved.

d)   a detailed scheme of marketing activities.

2.   An organizational mission is
    a)   what makes a company different from competition.
    b)   a clear, concise goal.
    c)   a means of organizing operations.
    d)   a quantifiable object.

3.   SBU stands for
    a)   small business undertaking.
    b)   smart business undertaking.
    c)   strategic business unit.
    d)   None of the above.

4.   A product that is classified as a "cash cow" by the BCG procedure
    a)   enjoys high market share but low levels of market growth.
    b)   has high market growth rate and high market share.
    c)   enjoys rapid growth but poor profit margins.
    d)   has both low market share and market growth.

5.   The Boston Consulting Group's portfolio matrix classifies products based on two dimensions:
    a)   profit last fiscal period and stock return.
    b)   competitive status and earnings potential.
    c)   relative market share and earnings potential.
    d)   None of the above.

6.   A product that is a "problem child"
    a)   enjoys high market share but low levels of market growth.
    b)   has high market growth rate and high market share.
    c)   enjoys rapid growth but poor profit margins.

Copyright © 1996 by Harcourt Brace & Company
All rights reserved.

d)   has a low market share but high market growth.

7.   Three brands—X,Y, and Z—constitute an industry for
        one product category. Their market shares are 50, 30, and
        20, respectively. Brand C's relative market share is
        a)   1.0.
        b)   0.67.
        c)   0.4.
        d)   None of the above.

8.   One of the products in your portfolio is a "star." Which
        of the following is *not* an appropriate action for this
        product?
        a)   Protect existing share by going after potential new
                product users.
        b)   Use excess cash to support development of new
                products.
        c)   Invest in product improvements.
        d)   All of the above are appropriate strategic actions.

9.   Which of the following is *not* a component of a marketing
        plan?
        a)   executive summary
        b)   creation of strategic plan objectives
        c)   assessment of opportunities and threats
        d)   preparation of action programs and budgets

10.   Which of the following is true regarding General
        Electric's Attractiveness/Strength portfolio model?
        a)   It classifies products or SBUs along three
                underlying dimensions.
        b)   It uses more information to classify products than
                does the Boston Consulting Group.
        c)   It is used exclusively for classifying financial
                investment products: stocks, bonds, mutual funds,
                etc.
        d)   All of the above are true.

Copyright © 1996 by Harcourt Brace & Company
All rights reserved.

11.   It is particularly appropriate to use a Survey of Executive
       Opinion for forecasting sales of
       a)   technologically innovative products.
       b)   products that compete under highly dynamic
             circumstances.
       c)   existing products with proven track records.
       d)   all of the above.

12.   Exponential smoothing gets its name from
       a)   the fact that this technique is used for forecasting
             products that have a past history of non-
             rollercoaster, or smooth, sales.
       b)   the use of a weighing factor, or smoothing
             constant, that is applied to past sales to forecast
             future sales.
       c)   the use of executive judgment in forecasting sales.
       d)   None of the above are correct.

13.   A product's sales revenue this year was $10,000,000,
       whereas it was forecast to have enjoyed sales of
       $11,000,000. Using exponential smoothing with an alpha
       of 0.3, what level of sales would be forecast for next
       year?
       a) $10,300,000
       b) $10,700,000
       c) $10,500,000
       d) $11,500,000

14.   Which is correct regarding the value of the smoothing
       constant, alpha, in exponential smoothing?
       a)   It typically is set between 0.1 and 0.5.
       b)   The higher the value of alpha, the greater the
             impact that past (versus recent) sales have on the
             present forecast.
       c)   The value of alpha and the impact of past and
             recent sales are unrelated.

Copyright © 1996 by Harcourt Brace & Company
All rights reserved.

d)   An alpha value of 0.3 is always the best, because this value is midway between the limits of 0.1 and 0.5.

15.   With reference to Sales and Marketing Management's multiple-factor index for estimating sales potential in a given market, which of the following factors is *not* included in this index.
a)   population
b)   disposable income
c)   retail sales
d)   number of competitive brands

Discussion Questions

1.   A startling merger for the communications industry was agreed to in 1995 between Disney and ABC/Cap Cities. From Disney's point of view, how might this merger fit into the strategic plans for the company?

2.   Working with the marketing mix variables is often thought of as tactical planning. Do you agree or disagree? What support can you give for your answer?

3.   What would you say is the mission of your college or university?

4.   Choose a popular restaurant located near your college or university. List the strengths and weaknesses that are characteristics of this restaurant; list opportunities and threats that it faces.

Copyright © 1996 by Harcourt Brace & Company
All rights reserved.

Chapter 8

Product Concepts and Strategies

Learning Objectives

1. Define product.

2. Distinguish between core, actual, and augmented product.

3. Explain the classifications of consumer and business-to-business products.

4. Distinguish between product mix and product line.

5. Explain what is meant by product mix width and product line depth.

6. Explain the advantages of offering multiple product lines.

7. Discuss the advantages of brand extension.

8. Describe the criteria for product elimination

9. Understand the strategic decisions in creating the actual product.

10. Explain the importance of various augmented product features.

Copyright © 1996 by Harcourt Brace & Company
All rights reserved.

Chapter Summary

A product is everything a buyer receives in an exchange with a seller. Products can be viewed at three different levels: the core product (consists of the key benefits that satisfy a consumer's need), the actual product (the core product plus the brand name, package, extra features, and quality level), and the augmented product (the actual product plus post-purchase services). When a consumer buys a product, he or she is purchasing the total product concept including everything that adds value to the seller's offering.

Products are classified as either consumer products (products purchased by a consumer for his or her own use) or business-to-business products (products purchased by an organization for use in business operations). Some can be classified as both a consumer and business-to-business product, since the classification is dependent on who buys the product and how it will be used.

Consumer products are further classified into categories based on how the consumer views and shops for the product. Consumer products are either convenience products, shopping products, specialty products, or unsought products. The product's price and purchase importance determine the level of involvement a consumer will devote to purchasing the product and, in turn, the amount, or intensity, of distribution a product must receive in order to be successful.

Business-to-business products are further classified into categories based on how the product will be used. Categories of business-to-business products include installations, accessories, raw materials, component parts/materials, supplies, and business-to-business services.

All of the products a company offers constitute its product mix. A group of related items is a product line. Multiple product lines enable a company to boost market growth and company profits.

Copyright © 1996 by Harcourt Brace & Company
All rights reserved.

The product lines must be periodically reviewed to determine whether the lines should be expanded or contracted.

In creating the actual product, a manager must make many decisions regarding the branding, packaging, and quality of the product. All of these features help to differentiate the product from its competitors. In creating an augmented product, the post-sale support features of delivery, installation, after-sale service, and warranties are features that differentiate the product from its competitors.

Chapter Exercises

Exercise 1

Choose a consumer durable good, such as a personal computer, that is sold through a variety of outlets. The outlets may include mass merchandisers, office supply stores, and mail order. Read promotional material and visit retail outlets to learn how each manufacturer and outlet combination augments their product. Write a report on your findings and discuss the strength and weakness of their strategies.

Exercise 2

Visit a local supermarket or mass merchandiser and look for three or four products with outstanding packaging features. Either write a description of the packaging or purchase the products for use as an example. Use the VIEW model to write an analysis of the packaging and be prepared to discuss your findings in class.

Chapter Review Questions

(Correct answers are listed in Appendix B.)

1.   A(n) _____ encompasses the key benefits consumers seek when making a purchase in the product category.
   a)   actual product
   b)   core product

Copyright © 1996 by Harcourt Brace & Company
All rights reserved.

c) augmented product

d) total product

2. Which of the following is *not* one of the various types of business-to business products?

a) contains the core product plus a brand name, a package, a desired quality level, symbolic features, and so on.

b) includes post-purchase services.

c) is comprised of the key benefits the product provides to the consumer.

d) is called an actual product in contrast to a service.

3. Which of the following is *not* one of the various types of business-to business products?

a) accessories

b) component parts/materials

c) installations

d) specialty items

4. A specialty product is

a) an inexpensive item that consumers purchase with little effort.

b) a particular brand in a product category that a consumer essentially insists on.

c) a known product that is not actually sought by consumers.

d) one that consumers find special due to nostalgia or other sentimental reasons for purchasing.

5. Business-to-business products are classified by

a) how a product will be used.

b) when a product will be used.

c) in what department a product will be used.

d) the type of business that purchases the product.

Copyright © 1996 by Harcourt Brace & Company
All rights reserved.

6. Which of the following is *not* a type of consumer product?
   a) convenience product
   b) shopping product
   c) installment product
   d) unsought product

7. A _____ constitutes all of the products an organization markets.
   a) product mix
   b) product line
   c) product extension
   d) product assortment

8. What is the simplest means of expanding a product line?
   a) By introducing an entirely new product.
   b) By offering a new size or feature to an existing product.
   c) By using a brand extension strategy.
   d) By acquiring a new brand from another company.

9. Which of the following is *not* an advantage of expanding a product line?
   a) Overall company sales and market share can increase.
   b) A company can become a single source of supply for its customers.
   c) Underutilized production capacity may be used.
   d) All of the above are advantages.

10. A product that is unknown to the customer or one that the consumer does not actively seek is called a(n) _____ product.
    a) unsought
    b) avoidance
    c) nonshopping
    d) None of the above

74

Copyright © 1996 by Harcourt Brace & Company
All rights reserved.

11. A brand mark is
    a) the unspoken characteristics of a brand such as a brand logo.
    b) that part of a brand consisting of words or letters that comprise a name used to identify the product.
    c) a brand that has been given legally protected status exclusive to the owner.
    d) the form of branding most often used in lesser developed countries where the illiteracy rate is high.

12. A private brand is
    a) one customized for a specific group of wealthy consumers.
    b) marketed exclusively to small grocery stores.
    c) a brand that is manufactured exclusively for a particular retailer and is not available to other retailers.
    d) typically premium priced in comparison to national brands.

13. A brand that has achieved a high level of brand loyalty due to its ability to satisfy consumers is said to possess
    a) a total product concept.
    b) brand equity.
    c) core benefits.
    d) augmentation.

14. Which of the following is *not* a component of the VIEW model of packaging?
    a) visibility
    b) information
    c) effectiveness
    d) workability

15. An example of an augmented product feature is

75

Copyright © 1996 by Harcourt Brace & Company
All rights reserved.

a)   the package.
b)   the brand name.
c)   the quality level.
d)   the warranty.

16.   A university builds a new indoor practice facility for the soccer team. This product would be classified as a(n)
a)   installation.
b)   accessory.
c)   component part.
d)   business-to-business service.

17.   There are various advantages to a firm's offering multiple products (rather than a single product). Which of the following is *not* one of these advantages.
a)   To offset fluctuations in sales.
b)   To achieve greater market impact.
c)   To avoid obsolescence.
d)   All of these are advantages.

18.   Expanding a product line offers several advantages to a company. Which of the following is *not* one of these advantages?
a)   A company can become a single source of supply for its customers with an expanded product line.
b)   Advertising costs can be spread over several products.
c)   Maintaining product quality is less important when a company has multiple products in its product line.
d)   More products mean more production to a facility that may be underutilizing its capacity.

19.   Although Jockey is the specific brand of a company that markets underwear, many people use the term jockey shorts to refer to a certain style of underwear rather than

Copyright © 1996 by Harcourt Brace & Company
All rights reserved.

to the brand per se. Hence, for these consumers the name Jockey has become

a)   preemptive.
b)   exemptive.
c)   restrictive.
d)   generic.

20.   Because brands sometimes have problems and even catastrophes, many companies avoid using the same family name for all brands in a particular product category. Thus, instead of using family branding, they prefer to use _____ branding.

a)   private
b)   national
c)   individual
d)   protective

21.   Which of the following descriptions best describes the practice of total quality management (TQM)?

a)   The total product concept is more than the sum of its parts.
b)   All components of a business enterprise should aim to produce the highest quality product in the industry.
c)   All departments in the organization need to be committed to the strategic goal of achieving quality.
d)   The production and engineering departments should determine the level of product quality a firm should offer.

22.   Which of the following is *not* an augmented product feature?

a)   delivery
b)   installation
c)   after-sale service
d)   packaging

Copyright © 1996 by Harcourt Brace & Company
All rights reserved.

Discussion Questions

1. Many products fall into different categories of the goods classification. How would you market a product as a shopping good and how would the marketing mix change for a specialty good?

2. How is a product different if it is viewed only as a core benefit versus a total product concept?

3. Discuss the pros and cons of creating a manufacturer's brand for your product.

4. Discuss packaging from the manufacturer's, wholesaler's, retailer's, and consumer's points of view.

Copyright © 1996 by Harcourt Brace & Company
All rights reserved.

Chapter 9

Product Development and Management

Learning Objectives

1. Name the ways a company can grow.

2. Discuss the market and product development strategies.

3. Describe the stages of the product life cycle.

4. Define brand-concept management.

5. Discuss the three categories of basic consumer needs.

6. Explain why companies need to continually develop new products.

7. Describe the structures used for new product development.

8. Discuss the six stages of the product life cycle.

9. Discuss the diffusion process and its consumers.

10. Describe the rate of adoption determinants.

11. Understand the process of product failure and elimination.

Copyright © 1996 by Harcourt Brace & Company
All rights reserved.

Chapter Summary

Growth is fundamental to a firm's success. Growth can only come by increasing sales of existing products in existing markets, entering new markets, or developing new products. A firm can choose from four basic market and product development strategies all designed to promote growth: market penetration, market development, product development, or product diversification.

All products go through a product life cycle, or a series of stages—market introduction, market growth, market maturity, sales decline—from inception until they are withdrawn from the market. The length of each stage and the entire life of the product will vary from product to product depending on new technologies, consumer dissatisfaction, or competitive activities.

The concept of the brand, or the specific meaning that is created for the brand and communicated to consumers, must be successfully managed throughout the brand's life cycle. A brand concept is created by promoting a brand as appealing predominantly to consumers' functional, symbolic, or experiential needs.

New-product development is a necessity for any firm that hopes to realize long-term success. Developing new products is a difficult, complex process involving many departments and resources within the organization. Since the efforts of so many are needed to successfully develop a new product, a coordinated, systematic approach is required throughout the process. Firms rely on new-product committees, new-product departments, venture teams, product managers, and cross-functional teams to coordinate new product activity. New products typically progress through six developmental stages: idea generation, screening, business analysis, development, testing, and commercialization.

Product diffusion is the process by which a new product spreads through the marketplace. Different consumers will behave

80

Copyright © 1996 by Harcourt Brace & Company
All rights reserved.

differently when a new product is introduced. The five categories of consumer behavior in the diffusion process are innovators, early adopters, early majority, late majority, and laggards. The rate at which a new product is adopted depends on the relative advantage, compatibility, complexity, trialability, and observability of the product.

All products must be periodically reviewed for their contribution to company objectives. Products that are not profitable must be eliminated from the product line so that the resources can be better applied to another product or marketing activity.

Chapter Exercises

Exercise 1

Choose a product category, such as perfumes or sodas, and search current magazines for ads promoting three or four different brands of the selected category. Clip or write a description of the ads and analyze the advertisers' efforts to create symbolic value for the different brands.. Write a report of your findings noting how the advertisers have positioned each of the brands.

Exercise 2

Go to a local electronics store or other durable good retailer and ask a salesperson to identify new products that they have recently received. Write a description of two or three of these products. Use the Rate-of-Adoption Determinant to evaluate the products and analyze how rapidly they will diffuse in the market place. Write a report of your findings.

Chapter Review Questions

(Correct answers are listed in Appendix B.)

1. Market penetration is a strategy that
    a) is used to increase market share with existing products in existing markets.

Copyright © 1996 by Harcourt Brace & Company
All rights reserved.

b)   involves finding new markets and new users for existing products.

c)   introduces new products into established markets.

d)   focuses on developing new products for new markets.

2.   Product development is a strategy that

a)   is used to increase market share with existing products in existing markets.

b)   involves finding new markets and new users for existing products.

c)   introduces new products into established markets.

d)   focuses on developing new products for new markets.

3.   A market development strategy

a)   is used to increase market share with existing products in existing markets.

b)   involves finding new markets and new users for existing products.

c)   introduces new products into established markets.

d)   focuses on developing new products for new markets.

4.   What dictates the length of a product's life cycle?

a)   new technologies

b)   consumer dissatisfaction

c)   competitive activities

d)   all of the above

5.   In the introduction stage of the product life cycle, the pioneering firm's top priority is to

a)   ensure the best possible level of quality.

b)   obtain distribution at retail and to inform customers about the product.

c)   iron out any problems in production and distribution.

Copyright © 1996 by Harcourt Brace & Company
All rights reserved.

d)   achieve maximum profits.

6.   During what stage in the product life cycle is the product
        the most *un*profitable?
        a)   introduction
        b)   growth
        c)   maturity
        d)   decline

7.   Sales revenues are maximized at what stage in the
        product life cycle?
        a)   introduction
        b)   growth
        c)   maturity
        d)   decline

8.   When a product pioneer introduces a new product with a
        relatively high price, it is adopting a(n)_____
        strategy.
        a)   penetration
        b)   exploitation
        c)   faulty
        d)   skimming

9.   Primary demand creation is emphasized at which stage in
        a product's life cycle?
        a)   introduction
        b)   growth
        c)   maturity
        d)   decline

10.   Brand-concept management is
        a)   the process of developing a new product idea.
        b)   the process of assigning a brand name to a
                product.
        c)   the marketing activities used during the
                introduction stage of a product's life cycle.

83
Copyright © 1996 by Harcourt Brace & Company
All rights reserved.

d)   the planning implementation, and control of a brand's meaning throughout its life.

11.   Appeals to consumers' symbolic needs are those involving
a)   current consumption-related problems.
b)   psychological needs.
c)   the desire for products that provide sensory pleasure, stimulation, and variety.
d)   imaginary needs.

12.   A manufacturer of bed sheeting advertises its product as the softest and most comfortable sheet in the industry. This company is appealing to consumers' _____ needs.
a)   symbolic
b)   experiential
c)   functional
d)   all of the above needs are being appealed to.

13.   What is the most common organizational structure for new product development?
a)   new-product committees
b)   venture teams
c)   new-product departments
d)   a cross-functional team

14.   The screening stage in the new-product development process is involved in
a)   viewing the package for the new product.
b)   identifying the most promising ideas and eliminating the rest.
c)   testing a prototype of a product that will be introduced to the market.
d)   analyzing the cost, revenue, and profit potential of product ideas.

84

Copyright © 1996 by Harcourt Brace & Company
All rights reserved.

15. In which stage of new product development are preliminary marketing strategies developed?
   a)   business analysis
   b)   idea generation
   c)   commercialization
   d)   development

16. In which stage of new product development are assessments made about a new product's market potential, growth rate, and financial funding?
   a)   business analysis
   b)   idea generation
   c)   commercialization
   d)   development

17. What is the diffusion process?
   a)   The process by which a consumer retains information about a product.
   b)   The process by which new ideas spread through a social system or marketplace.
   c)   The time it takes for a new product to be developed and introduced to the market.
   d)   The process by which new products are eliminated from the marketplace.

18. What group will spend more time deciding whether or not to try a new product than any other group in the diffusion process?
   a)   early majority
   b)   innovators
   c)   early adopters
   d)   late majority

19. Which group of adopters are particularly important in their role as opinion leaders?
   a)   innovators
   b)   early adopters

Copyright © 1996 by Harcourt Brace & Company
All rights reserved.

c)   early majority

d)   late majority

20.   A manufacturer of golf clubs touted its product as having a unique metal alloy unlike any other club on the market stating that this feature would promote greater distance. Consumers, however, could not see the alloy when inspecting the clubs in the store, and hence they were not eager to purchase this new product. In terms of factors that facilitate more rapid product adoption, this product could be said to lack

a)   a relative advantage.

b)   trialability.

c)   observability.

d)   important symbolism.

Discussion Questions

1. Discuss the advantages of product development versus market development.

2. Using a new product, such as the CD-ROM version of this book, discuss the potential marketing mix changes throughout the life cycle of the product.

3. Discuss potential criteria for a hypothetical company to use during each of the stages of the new product development process.

4. When should products be eliminated from a company's portfolio?

Copyright © 1996 by Harcourt Brace & Company
All rights reserved.

Chapter 10

Marketing Channels and Distribution

Learning Objectives

1. Define the functions of Marketing channels and physical distribution.

2. Describe the roles of channel intermediaries.

3. Demonstrate business to business channels.

4. Demonstrate consumer channels.

5. Define Vertical marketing systems.

6. Discuss channel dynamics.

7. Review legal considerations.

8. Analyze the various forms of physical distribution.

Chapter Summary

Distribution, the function that makes products available to consumers, is a critical component of any product's marketing mix. A channel of distribution is the arrangement of businesses that are involved in performing marketing functions and physically transferring goods and services and their ownership from manufacturers to end-users. Physical distribution is the aspect of marketing that physically moves and stores products as

Copyright © 1996 by Harcourt Brace & Company
All rights reserved.

they flow through the channel of distribution. The objective of physical distribution is getting the right product to the right place at the right time.

Marketing intermediaries, all of the business institutions that facilitate the exchange process between buyers and seller, play a crucial role in effecting exchanges in the marketplace. Various types of intermediaries in the marketplace include wholesalers, retailers, brokers, and distributors. Intermediaries are needed to reduce the number of contacts between manufacturers and end-users, provide a solution to the discrepancies of quantity and assortment, and share marketing functions with the manufacturer and other channel members.

Various channels of distribution exist to perform the marketing functions needed to distribute the vast number of products in the marketplace. Business-to-business channel structures differ from consumer channels. Business-to-business channel structures use agents/brokers or distributors to reach the end-user. Consumer channel structures either deal directly with retailers or utilize wholesalers and/or brokers to reach the wholesaler and retailers. Many companies utilize more than one channel for distributing their products. The number of channels used depends on the whether the company wishes to achieve intensive, selective, or exclusive distribution.

There has been a steady trend in the era of modern marketing toward unified channel arrangements, also called vertical marketing systems (VMSs). In VMSs, channel members cooperate with each other and join forces to effectively and efficiently reach the entire channel's target market. Channel members attempt to share, control, or combine channel functions. The three basic types of VMSs are corporate, contractual, and administered systems.

Marketers must be aware of the issues of power, conflict, and leadership within the channel so every effort can be made to ensure that the highest level of cooperation is maintained.

Copyright © 1996 by Harcourt Brace & Company
All rights reserved.

Channel management must be aware of the laws and regulations that affect every aspect of their business.

Channel members perform exchange functions and also the physical distribution functions of buying and selling. Physical distribution includes those activities that get the right products to the right places at the right times to satisfy consumer needs such as receiving and processing orders, storing and controlling inventories, transporting products, and servicing customers. Physical distribution functions are interrelated and must be viewed as a whole rather than in fragmented parts to minimize the firm's costs. An organization's objective should be to offer the best possible service to its customers at the lowest possible cost.

Chapter Exercises

Exercise 1

Choose three product categories that represent each of the following distribution intensities: intensive, selective, and exclusive. Visit retail stores and observe the chosen items and the differences in their marketing. Write a report of your observations and evaluate the appropriateness of the marketing strategies from a distribution point of view.

Exercise 2

During the 1980s and early 1990s, a trend toward unified channel arrangements occurred. These arrangements, referred to as vertical marketing systems and strategic alliances, have three basic designs—corporate, contractual, and administered systems. Search electronic databases in your library for articles that describe recent alliances. Choose an alliance and write a report detailing the activity and the proposed advantages that accrue to the parties. Recent examples of alliances include the ABC/Cap City and Disney, and the Time Warner and Turner mergers.

Copyright © 1996 by Harcourt Brace & Company
All rights reserved.

Chapter Review Questions

(Correct answers are listed in Appendix B.)

1.   A marketing intermediary that takes title to products for resale is called a
    a)   merchant middleman.
    b)   functional middleman.
    c)   title merchant.
    d)   warehouse operator

2.   Generally speaking, which of the following economic roles is *not* performed by marketing intermediaries?
    a)   Intermediaries reduce the number of transactions in an exchange process.
    b)   They provide a solution to the discrepancy of quantity between manufacturers and end users.
    c)   They provide a solution to the discrepancy of assortment between manufacturers and end users.
    d)   They increase the cost of marketing

3.   Which of the following is *not* a traditional channel arrangement for marketing business-to-business products in the United States?
    a)   Producer–>Business Customers
    b)   Producer–>Agents/Brokers–>Business Customers
    c)   Producer–>Retailers–>Business Customers
    d)   Producer–>Distributors–>Business Customers

4.   An agent that performs only a selling function for the producers they represent is called a(n)
    a)   selling agent.
    b)   salesperson.
    c)   distributor.
    d)   manufacturer's agent.

5.   An agent that performs marketing functions other than just selling for the producers they represent is called a(n)

90

Copyright © 1996 by Harcourt Brace & Company
All rights reserved.

a) selling agent.
b) salesperson.
c) distributor.
d) manufacturer's agent.

6. Which of the following channel arrangements is *not* used in the marketing of consumer goods?
   a) Producer–>Consumer
   b) Producer–>Retailer–>Wholesaler–>Consumer
   c) Producer–>Agents/Brokers–> Retailers–>Consumers
   d) Producer–>Agents/Brokers–> Wholesalers–>Retailers–>Consumers

7. A small manufacturer produces novelty products that are carried in small retail grocery stores in rural parts of the United States. Which of the following is the most probable channel of distribution for this manufacturer's products?
   a) Producer–>Consumer
   b) Producer–>Retailer–>Wholesaler–>Consumer
   c) Producer–>Wholesaler–>Consumers
   d) Producer–>Agents/Brokers–> Wholesalers–>Retailers–>Consumers

8. Which of the following statements is *false* regarding intensive distribution.
   a) Intensive distribution is used when a product is sold in virtually every available retail outlet in a particular market.
   b) Products that require extensive after-sale service are distributed intensively.
   c) Convenience products such as soft drinks and candy are likely candidates for intensive distribution.
   d) None of the above are false.

Copyright © 1996 by Harcourt Brace & Company
All rights reserved.

9. Which of the following statements is most likely to be true?
   a) Exclusive distribution occurs when a manufacturer markets its product directly to consumers, which gives the manufacturer exclusive control of its product.
   b) Intensive distribution occurs when a manufacturer sells directly to millions of consumers in an intensive effort to maximize profits.
   c) Selective distribution is practiced when a manufacturer distributes its product through few retail outlets in each market.
   d) Exclusive distribution is unethical and illegal.

10. Which of the following vertical marketing systems is characterized by a rather loose relationship among channel members and control by a channel captain?
   a) Corporate VMS
   b) Administered VMS
   c) Contractual VMS
   d) Forward-integrated VMS

11. A company that historically has been only a manufacturer recently opened its own outlets to retail the products it manufactures. This practice is called
   a) a vertical marketing system.
   b) backward integration.
   c) forward integration.
   d) an administered vertical marketing system.

12. Which of the following statements is false regarding contractual vertical marketing systems?
   a) Franchises are a form of contractual VMS.
   b) Voluntary chains are sponsored by retailers.
   c) Cooperative chains are sponsored by retailers.
   d) Contractual VMSs are illegal.

Copyright © 1996 by Harcourt Brace & Company
All rights reserved.

13.   When a manufacturer attempts to prohibit a wholesaler or retailer from handling competitive product lines, this practice is called
        a)   selective distribution.
        b)   discriminatory merchandising.
        c)   exclusive distribution.
        d)   exclusive dealing.

14.   Which of the following statements is true regarding tying agreements?
        a)   Tying agreement: when a retail salesperson convinces consumers to buy a second product after buying a first.
        b)   A manufacturer is using a tying agreement when it refuses to sell one product to a retailer unless the retailer purchases another product from the manufacturer.
        c)   Tying agreements occur between competitive retailers; e.g., when one retailer convinces a competitor that both should increase prices.
        d)   Tying agreements are always illegal.

15.   Which of the following activities is *not* considered part of physical distribution
        a)   Receiving and processing orders.
        b)   Determining which retailers should be allowed to handle the manufacturer's products.
        c)   Transporting and storage.
        d)   Servicing customers.

16.   The economic order quantity (EOQ) occurs when
        a)   carrying and ordering costs are equal.
        b)   carrying costs are minimized.
        c)   ordering costs are minimized.
        d)   When both carrying costs and ordering costs are individually minimized.

Copyright © 1996 by Harcourt Brace & Company
All rights reserved.

17. Which of the following statements is false regarding just-in-time ordering and electronic data interchange?
  a) JIT is used by manufacturers when purchasing component parts from suppliers.
  b) JIT was first used in Japan.
  c) EDI involves the sharing and exchange of information between retailers and their suppliers.
  d) EDI involves the sharing and exchange of information between manufacturers and their trade associations.

Discussion Questions

1. Motorola, a manufacturer of audio equipment for automobiles, sells equipment to manufacturers where it is factory-installed in automobiles and to dealers where it is custom-installed for consumers. Discuss the differences in the channels of distribution required to serve the two markets.

2. Most items found in a hardware store are sold through a series of intermediaries such as a full-service wholesaler. What services do these intermediaries provide to justify the markup that adds to the price of the products for the hardware store?

3. What are the characteristics of a consumer product that would suggest a "long" channel would be the appropriate method of distribution?

4. A number of consumer products companies (e.g., Amway, Avon, and Mary Kay Cosmetics) have established impressive sales growth through direct marketing. What factors have led to this success? (For a contrast, review your answer to Question 3.)

Copyright © 1996 by Harcourt Brace & Company
All rights reserved.

Chapter 11

Wholesaling and Retailing

Learning Objectives

1. Discuss the number and types of wholesalers.

2. Discuss the number and types of retailers.

3. Analyze new trends in retailing.

4. Describe types of nonstore retailing.

5. Discuss the evolution of retailing.

6. Analyze the future of retailing.

Chapter Summary

Manufacturers cannot perform all of the necessary channel functions to get the right product to the right place at the right time. These functions can be shared among channel intermediaries, but they cannot be eliminated. Wholesalers and retailers help manufacturers market consumer products to consumers. Industrial distributors and agents help manufacturers market business-to-business products to customers.

Wholesalers are an integral part of all marketing systems. Wholesalers are individuals or organizations that help in providing time, place, and possession utilities to business-to-business customers and retailers. Many different types of wholesalers exist to meet the unique needs of the diverse group

95

Copyright © 1996 by Harcourt Brace & Company
All rights reserved.

of retailers and producers in operation in today's marketplace. There are three general forms of wholesaling intermediaries each distinguished by their specialized activities. The manufacturer's sales offices and branches are owned and operated by manufacturers. A merchant wholesaler is an intermediary that purchases, takes title to goods, and assumes all risks associated with ownership. Merchant wholesalers can be either full-service—including general merchandise, limited line, specialty line, or industrial distributors—or limited service—including rack jobbers, truck jobbers, drop shippers, cash and carry wholesalers, or mail-order wholesalers. Agents and brokers provide the buying and selling channel functions but do not take title to the products they sell. As producers become more marketing-oriented, so, too, have wholesalers. Today's wholesalers are attempting to satisfy the needs of both the producers they represent and the customers they serve.

Retailing encompasses those activities involved in the exchange process of goods and services to the final consumer. Retailing is a dynamic enterprise that is constantly changing in advanced economies. Retailers differ greatly in terms of how they choose to operate and where they place their strategic emphasis. Product lines and assortments, service quality, atmospherics, and price levels and margins are just some of the strategic tools that enable retailers to differentiate themselves from competitors and meet consumers' needs.

The retailing industry is highly diverse, consisting of the following retail types: specialty stores, outlet malls, department stores, and general merchandise outlets, including membership clubs, hypermarkets, warehouse and catalog showrooms, and home improvement centers.

Many marketers today, though, are finding a niche by selling to consumers through nonstore retailing, or selling products and services outside of conventional retail outlets. Several trends such as catalog marketing, telemedia, direct selling, automatic merchandising, and electronic retailing in the marketplace are

Copyright © 1996 by Harcourt Brace & Company
All rights reserved.

seeing more out-of-store and in-home buying. Retailing practices are continuously changing because of competitive pressures, technological developments, and societal changes.

Chapter Exercises

Exercise 1

Visit a local retailer and talk with someone who purchases merchandise for the store. Ask the buyer to describe the types of distributors that supply his or her store and the services that are provided by the distributors. Write a report from your findings and include a chart of the channels that are used to supply the store.

Exercise 2

Visit your favorite retail store and make notes of its atmospherics—include exterior and interior aspects. In a written report describe the store and how the atmospherics position the store and influence customers' behavior.

Chapter Review Questions

(Correct answers are listed in Appendix B.)

1. As a form of wholesaling, a manufacturer's sales office
   a) is always located at the production facility.
   b) operates like an independent agent.
   c) carries inventory.
   d) All of the above are correct.

2. Which is *not* a full-service wholesaler?
   a) rack jobber
   b) specialty line wholesaler
   c) general merchandise wholesaler
   d) limited line wholesaler

3. How do limited-service merchant wholesalers differ from full-service merchant wholesalers?

97

Copyright © 1996 by Harcourt Brace & Company
All rights reserved.

a)   Limited-service wholesalers do not take title to the goods.
b)   Limited-service wholesalers do not store products.
c)   Limited-service wholesalers offer a narrower range of support services.
d)   Limited-service wholesalers offer higher prices than full-service wholesalers.

4.   Drop shippers
    a)   are wholesaling intermediaries that sell products, take orders, and arrange for delivery of products.
    b)   do not store, handle, or deliver any of the products they sell.
    c)   offer little or no promotional assistance to their retail customers.
    d)   All of the above are accurate descriptions of drop shippers.

5.   Agents and brokers
    a)   do not take title to the products they sell.
    b)   always represent buyers instead of sellers.
    c)   are virtually useless as marketing intermediaries because they do not maintain inventories.
    d)   take title to the products they sell.

6.   Wholesaling entities that supply products to retailers and the display units on which the products are displayed are called
    a)   full-service merchant wholesalers.
    b)   drop shippers.
    c)   truck jobbers.
    d)   rack jobbers.

7.   Which of the following statements is false regarding drop shippers.
    a)   They also are called desk jobbers.

Copyright © 1996 by Harcourt Brace & Company
All rights reserved.

b) They take orders and arrange for delivery of products directly to customers.
c) They are typically used in high-tech industries such as computers and communications equipment.
d) They are typically involved in the marketing of products that have high shipping costs.

8. Which type of agent effectively represents the marketing department for the manufacturer it represents?
a) selling agents
b) marketing agents
c) merchandise agents
d) manufacturer's agents

9. Which of the following is *not* a key feature of service quality?
a) reliability
b) suitability
c) responsiveness
d) accessibility

10. The practice of designing retailing environments that have emotional effects on shoppers and enhance their purchase probability is termed
a) emotion engineering.
b) retail entertronics.
c) Atmospherics.
d) all of the above.

11. Hypermarkets
a) are warehouse operations featuring all products used in the home.
b) are discount retailers that offer brand-name electronic and telecommunications merchandise at low prices.
c) are mass merchandisers and food stores combined.

99

Copyright © 1996 by Harcourt Brace & Company
All rights reserved.

d)   are full-service wholesalers.

12.   Which is *not* a form of nonstore retailing?
       a)   catalog marketing
       b)   telemedia
       c)   direct merchandising
       d)   outlet malls

13.   The wheel of retailing hypothesis
       a)   describes how retail institutions evolve from low-
               priced, low-service to higher-priced and higher-
               serviced operations.
       b)   explains why nonstore retailing will eventually
               eliminate all conventional forms of store retailing.
       c)   describes the flow of products through channel
               intermediaries.
       d)   occurs when a retailer adds product lines that are
               unrelated to its traditional product offerings.

14.   A form of specialty store that offers a large assortment of
       products within a limited number of product lines a
       discount prices is called a
       a)   category killer.
       b)   hypermarket.
       c)   scrambled merchandiser.
       d)   department store.

15.   Which of the following is false regarding department
       stores?
       a)   They offer a wide range of product lines with
               some depth in each line.
       b)   They are divided into separate departments each
               offering related products.
       c)   They are experiencing a more rapid rate of sales
               growth than any other form of retail institution in
               the U.S.

100

Copyright © 1996 by Harcourt Brace & Company
All rights reserved.

d)   They have been hurt by the movement of the population to the suburbs.

16.   _____occurs when a retail establishment veers away from its original marketing strategy and adds product lines that are unrelated to the retailer's original product offering.
a)   Mass merchandising
b)   Scrambled merchandising
c)   Wheel-of-retailing merchandising
d)   Hyper merchandising

Discussion Questions

1. What merchandising trends that are taking place in today's economy threaten wholesalers? What are wholesalers doing to counter these trends?

2. Discuss the major differences between a full-service and a limited-service wholesaler.

3. What are the key features of service quality that retailers must observe in order to survive in today's competitive environment? Provide examples of good and bad retailer practices with regard to these features.

4. How can retailers insure that they are maintaining a level of quality that is satisfactory to their customers?

Copyright © 1996 by Harcourt Brace & Company
All rights reserved.

Chapter 12

Pricing Concepts and Determination

Learning Objectives

1. Discuss the various terms used for pricing.

2. Analyze the consumer's perspective on pricing.

3. Analyze the seller's perspective on pricing.

4. Discuss elasticity and pricing.

5. Review pricing and competitive structures.

6. Discuss the legal issues surrounding the pricing decision.

7. Describe demand considerations of pricing.

8. Describe cost considerations of pricing.

Chapter Summary

Of all the marketing mix variables, price is the most dynamic, unique, and perhaps the most important. Price can be thought of as the amount that buyer and seller agree on to exchange a product or service for money or another product or service. There are a variety of terms for price, but by any name price represents an exchange rate.

Copyright © 1996 by Harcourt Brace & Company
All rights reserved.

From the consumer's perspective, price plays both negative and positive roles—negative in the sense that price represents an outlay of economic resources, but positive in the sense that consumers sometimes infer quality from prices: higher prices often suggest higher quality and better products. Research shows that consumers use price as a signal of product quality when risk reduction is important in making purchases, when objective quality is difficult to assess, when consumers lack expertise, and when they are relatively uninvolved in the purchase situation. Consumers use reference prices to judge product offerings. Products priced at levels that exceed the consumer's latitude of acceptance are subject to rejection.

Five sets of factors are considered by marketing managers when setting prices: demand, which sets a ceiling on the price that can be charged; costs, which set a floor; competitive factors, which act to reduce the price ceiling; marketing objectives, which establish financial requirements for product prices; and regulatory constraints and ethical considerations, which limit a price setter's discretion.

The type of market structure—whether pure competition, pure monopoly, oligopolistic, or monopolistic competitive—plays an important role in determining price elasticity and thus the price setter's pricing freedom. Price elasticity, which measures customer responsiveness to price changes, is highly elastic in pure competition, highly inelastic in pure monopoly, and varies from elastic to inelastic in monopolistically competitive and oligopolistic market structures. In the latter situation, the demand curve is presumed to be kinked at the prevailing market price such that price elasticity above the prevailing price is elastic and inelastic below the price. In either event, the price setter faces potential loss in total revenues when unilaterally increasing or decreasing prices.

Pricing legislation has been enacted to prevent four untoward pricing practices: (1) price fixing, (2) predatory pricing, (3) price discrimination, and (4) dumping. Some of the more notable

Copyright © 1996 by Harcourt Brace & Company
All rights reserved.

legislative acts that prevent these practices are the Sherman Act, the Federal Trade Commission Act, the Clayton Act, and the Robinson-Patman Act. The latter act is particularly important in its efforts to prevent price discrimination. Charging unequal prices to competitive sellers is evidence of price discrimination, but the Robinson-Patman Act specifies situations when price discrimination is and is not unlawful.

In theory, prices should be set so that profits are maximized. Marginal analysis from economics provides a simple yet eloquent procedure for setting profit-maximizing prices. To use this approach, the price setter must determine marginal costs and marginal revenues associated with different price and quantity combinations. Then a profit maximizing price is determined by identifying that price-quantity combination where marginal revenue equals marginal cost. In practice it is virtually impossible to construct demand schedules, and it is for this reason that profit-maximizing pricing is more a theoretical ideal than practical reality.

Price setting in practice depends more on cost estimation rather than on demand estimation. Prices typically are set by both manufacturers and retailers using some form of cost-plus pricing method. In the case of manufacturers, target return pricing is especially prevalent. This method requires the price setter to add a desired rate of return on invested capital to the full cost of producing and marketing a product. Retailers typically set prices by simply adding a markup to product cost or to the selling price. The markup represents an amount that is sufficient for recovering costs and returning an adequate profit. Breakeven analysis is an especially valuable tool for initiating the price-determination process. The breakeven point is achieved when the contemplated price yields no profit or loss. Price setters can "play" with different prices and sales forecasts to identify a relevant range of pricing options.

Copyright © 1996 by Harcourt Brace & Company
All rights reserved.

Chapter Exercises

Exercise 1

This exercise tests the theory that price is an indicator of quality. Purchase three brands of inexpensive, but essentially equal, ball-point pens (you may use a different product). Establish fictitious prices for the pens—prices that are high, medium, and low.

Approach five or six of your friends, one at a time, and ask how they would rank the three pens on quality from best to worst. (Your subjects should include individuals who are *not* familiar with the price/quality relationship of your project.)

Make sure that the subjects know your *established* prices. Have the subjects try each pen. Record their rankings from best to worst and write a report of your findings noting whether the theory was upheld.

Exercise 2

From time to time, dumping becomes an issue in the popular press as foreign companies attempt to gain market share in the United States. Search electronically in your library for articles on dumping issues. In a written report, summarize one or two of the articles and comment on whether the dumping was verified and who lost or benefited from the practice.

Chapter Review Questions

(Correct answers are listed in Appendix B.)

1. Which of the following statements is false regarding price?
   a) Price represents an exchange rate.
   b) A product's price represents a quid pro quo between buyer and seller.
   c) Prices always are quoted and charged in monetary terms.
   d) None of the above are false.

Copyright © 1996 by Harcourt Brace & Company
All rights reserved.

2.   Price is likely to be used by consumers as an indicator, or signal, of product quality in all of the following situations except statement _____.
        a)   The consumer feels a need to reduce perceived purchase risk by selecting a brand that is of sufficient quality.
        b)   Objective product quality is easy for consumers to assess.
        c)   Consumers lack the ability to assess objective quality.
        d)   Consumers are relatively uninvolved in the purchase situation.

3.   Which of the following is true regarding reference prices?
        a)   Internal reference prices refer to price information possessed by and protected by retailers.
        b)   External reference prices are stored in the consumer's memory and are based on particular product category prices.
        c)   Internal reference prices are stored in the consumer's memory and are based on knowledge about prices in a particular product category.
        d)   Consumers who are frequent purchasers in a product category possess a wide range of price acceptability.

4.   Which of the following is *not* a recognized pricing objective?
        a)   cash flow and survival
        b)   profit maximization
        c)   target return on investment
        d)   break-even analysis

5.   At an initial price (P_1) of $10, a firm sold 1,000 units (Q_1) of Product X. At an increased price (P_2) of $12, the firm sold 900 units (Q_2) of Product X. Price elasticity in this situation is _____ .

106

Copyright © 1996 by Harcourt Brace & Company
All rights reserved.

a)   elastic
b)   inelastic
c)   unitary
d)   both elastic and inelastic

6.   At an initial price (P_1) of $10, a firm sold 1,000 units (Q_1) of Product X. An increased price (P_2) of $12, the firm sold 700 units (Q_2) of Product X. Price elasticity in this situation is _____ .
    a)   elastic
    b)   inelastic
    c)   unitary
    d)   both elastic and inelastic

7.   The kinked demand curve represents which market structure?
    a)   pure competition
    b)   pure monopoly
    c)   monopolistic competition
    d)   oligopoly

8.   Which of the following statements is false regarding elasticity of demand?
    a)   The demand curve in pure competition is perfectly elastic.
    b)   The demand curve in a pure monopoly is perfectly inelastic.
    c)   When price elasticity is elastic, an increase in price will result in an increase in total revenue.
    d)   When price elasticity is inelastic, an increase in price will result in an increase in total revenue.

9.   When two or more companies collude in some fashion to artificially maintain or set prices, this is called _____ .
    a)   dumping
    b)   predatory pricing
    c)   price fixing

Copyright © 1996 by Harcourt Brace & Company
All rights reserved.

d)   monopolistic activity

10.   When a firm sets a price in the short-term that is below its cost only later to raise its price to a very high level and earn exorbitant profits, this is called _____.
a)   dumping
b)   predatory pricing
c)   price fixing
d)   monopolistic activity

11.   The _____ Act is the primary legislation that is applied in cases of price discrimination.
a)   Sherman
b)   Robinson-Patman
c)   Miller-Tydings
d)   Federal Trade Commission

12.   There are various situations where charging different prices to competitive customers is legally permissible and not in violation of price-discrimination legislation. Which is *not* one of these?
a)   There is no harm to competition.
b)   The price-setter needs to charge differential prices in order to maximize its profits.
c)   Differential prices are charged to match a competitor's lower prices.
d)   Changes in interim market conditions justify charging differential prices.

13.   Which of the following statements in incorrect regarding cost concepts?
a)   Variable costs are fixed in total but variable per unit.
b)   Fixed costs are fixed in total but variable per unit.
c)   Marginal revenue is the change in total revenue associated with selling an additional item.

Copyright © 1996 by Harcourt Brace & Company
All rights reserved.

d)   Marginal cost is the change in total cost associated with selling an additional item.

14.   The rule for profit maximization is
    a)   increase prices until costs go down.
    b)   set prices at the particular price-quantity combination where total revenue equals total costs.
    c)   set prices at the particular price-quantity combination where total revenue is just slightly less than total cost.
    d)   set prices at the particular price-quantity combination where marginal revenue is equal to marginal costs.

15.   A firm's fixed cost for a particular product is $5,000,000. Its unit variable cost is $10. With a contemplated price of $15, how many units must be sold for the firm to break even?
    a)   100,000
    b)   20,000,000
    c)   1,000,000
    d)   Not enough information is provided.

16.   The break-even amount expressed in dollars in the previous question is
    a) $1,500,000.
    b) $35,000,000.
    c) $15,000,000.
    d)   Not enough information is provided.

17.   A retailer purchases an umbrella for $7 and sells it for $12. The markup on selling price in this case is
    a)   approximately 71%.
    b)   140%.
    c)   Approximately 42%.
    d)   240%.

Copyright © 1996 by Harcourt Brace & Company
All rights reserved.

18. If a retailer's markup on selling price is 35%, the equivalent markup on cost is
   a) approximately 25%.
   b) approximately 54%.
   c) approximately 75%.
   d) approximately 46%.

Discussion Questions

1. What factors cause a marketing textbook to lose value during the period of one semester. It is not unusual for a student to receive less than one-half of the purchase price when he or she sells the textbook at the end of the semester.

2. If two nearly identical wrist watches—except for brand name—have different prices, consumers generally conclude that the higher priced watch is of higher quality. What factors lead to this conclusion?

3. You are in a supermarket shopping for soda and other party items. A six-pack of Pepsi on a special display is priced at $5.95. Using the concept of reference prices, how would you and other consumers determine whether this is a good value?

4. Bob Martin, a local information technology manager, is prepared to build high quality desktop computers that would compete favorably with Dell Computers in a direct-mail market. He estimates annual fixed costs of $600,000 and variable costs of $1,800 per unit if he were to establish a production capacity of 100 units per month. Bob feels confident of selling 100 units per month. Should he take on this business? What price should he charge? (Assume a comparable Dell computer

Copyright © 1996 by Harcourt Brace & Company
All rights reserved.

Chapter 13

Pricing Strategies and Approaches

<table>
<tr><td colspan="2">Learning Objectives</td></tr>
<tr><td>1.</td><td>Discuss new product pricing policies.</td></tr>
<tr><td>2.</td><td>Define the various types of discounts and allowances.</td></tr>
<tr><td>3.</td><td>Analyze the concepts of price lining and bundling.</td></tr>
<tr><td>4.</td><td>Discuss psychological pricing strategies.</td></tr>
<tr><td>5.</td><td>Discuss geographic pricing strategies.</td></tr>
<tr><td>6.</td><td>Analyze price bidding strategies.</td></tr>
</table>

Chapter Summary

Price setters make a variety of pricing decisions beyond merely establishing the base price for a product. These decisions, or pricing strategies, include new-product pricing, price-flexibility strategies, discount and allowance strategies, product-line pricing, psychological pricing, geographic pricing strategies, and bid pricing.

Product pioneers have two general pricing options: skimming or penetration pricing. Skimming pricing involves charging relatively high prices and supporting this strategy with heavy promotional expenditures. Skimming pricing is most appropriate when price elasticity is inelastic and high initial prices are

Copyright © 1996 by Harcourt Brace & Company
All rights reserved.

necessary to recoup quickly the heavy investment in a new product. Penetration prices involve the use of relatively low prices because price elasticity is elastic, strong competition is imminent, and production costs can be substantially reduced if greater volume is achieved.

Manufacturers often adopt a flexible-pricing strategy by varying discounts and allowances on a transactional basis. Manufacturers typically flex the transaction amount as dictated by economic, competitive, and other marketplace circumstances. Pricing flexibility is constrained, however, by pricing restrictions imposed by the Robinson-Patman Act. At the retail level, price flexing occurs when price haggling transpires between retailer and customer. Haggling is commonplace throughout most of the world, but is less prevalent in more economically developed economies.

A variety of discounts and allowances are used in flexing prices and accommodating the specific circumstances surrounding a particular exchange situation. These include (1) functional, or trade, discounts; (2) quantity discounts, both cumulative and noncumulative; (3) seasonal discounts; (4) cash discounts; (5) sales promotion allowances such as price-off, bill-back, and slotting allowances; (6) trade-in allowances; (7) cash discounts; and (8) rebates.

Product-line pricing strategies are necessitated when manufacturers produce multiple brands in the same product category and when retailers merchandise multiple product-quality levels in the same category. The pricing issue faced both by manufacturers and retailers is one of whether to price each product in a line separately on the basis of its own cost, demand, and competitive characteristics or to jointly price the multiple products in recognition of the overall image that the firm wishes to convey and the interrelated demand, or cross elasticity, between the products. A related situation occurs when firms bundle two or more products or services in the same unit at a

Copyright © 1996 by Harcourt Brace & Company
All rights reserved.

special price, which typically is below the price of the components priced separately.

Three psychological-based pricing practices—prestige pricing, odd-even pricing, and loss-leader pricing—are prevalent in retailing. Prestige pricing is used when a product is priced at a relatively high price under the assumption that the relation between price and quantity demanded is direct rather than inverse, which means greater quantities will be sold at higher rather than lower prices. Odd-pricing, as contrasted with even-pricing, occurs when the end digits of a price use odd numbers (3, 5, 7, 9) or when the price is just below a whole number (e.g., $9.98 instead of $10.00). Price setters, when using odd-pricing, operate under the assumption that such prices convey a deal to consumers. Even-pricing, on the other hand, can be used to convey a prestige, high-quality image. Loss-leader pricing is practiced by retailers when an item is priced below or near cost to draw people to the store in anticipation that while there they will purchase other items, thus yielding an overall profit to the retailer.

Geographic pricing strategies are used when freight charges play an important role in the overall, or delivered, price of a product. FOB origin pricing charges the cost of transportation to customers. The amount depends on the volume shipped and the distance separating the customer and the seller's shipping point, with longer distances typically entailing higher costs. Uniform delivered pricing, a variant of FOB origin pricing, simply charges all customers the same, average shipping charge. Zone pricing is a special case of uniform delivered pricing where the seller divides the total territory into multiple zones and bills the same average shipping charge in each zone.

However, customers sometimes refuse to purchase from sellers unless the seller is willing to pay all or a portion of the transportation costs. Hence, FOB destination pricing, where the seller absorbs the freight charges, is used in highly competitive situations, especially where industry characteristics are such that

Copyright © 1996 by Harcourt Brace & Company
All rights reserved.

sellers have high fixed-cost and relatively low variable-cost structures. Basing-point pricing is a special case of FOB origin pricing. With this practice, freight charges are billed to the customer based on the cost of freight from a basing point (such as a competitor's shipping point) rather than the seller's actual shipping point. Basing-point pricing removes geographical monopolies and allows sellers to extend their markets.

Bid pricing addresses a different issue, namely the matter of pricing a product, project, or service on a one-time, bid-by-bid basis. Effective bid pricing requires that companies accurately estimate all cost components, have a good idea of how competitors might bid on a project, and build in a reasonable profit margin but not one that is too high to lose the bid to a competitive bidder.

Chapter Exercises

Exercise 1

Visit one or two retail stores in your local community to find and record instances of price lining. In a written report of your findings, discuss the types of products for which price lining does not work. Suggestion: For good results start with an appliance store or an electronics store.

Exercise 2

Work with your instructor to arrange a classroom visit by the manager of a wholesale distributor from your area. Ask the manager to discuss the various pricing arrangements between the wholesaler and manufacturers, and the wholesaler and retailers. Also have the manager describe the services that are provided by the wholesaler for other member of the trade.

Chapter Review Questions

(Correct answers are listed in Appendix B.)

Copyright © 1996 by Harcourt Brace & Company
All rights reserved.

1. A skimming price would be justified in all of the following circumstances except the following situation:
    a) Price elasticity is elastic.
    b) Price elasticity is inelastic.
    c) A product innovator wants to quickly recoup the heavy investment in a new product.
    d) The innovator realizes that product innovators and early adopters are relatively price insensitive.

2. Price haggling is most likely under all of the following circumstances except the following:
    a) Consumers' prior purchasing experience has provided them with a reference point of what the fair price should be.
    b) The asking price is perceived as unreasonable.
    c) Consumers know that prices for comparable products differ among sellers.
    d) All of the above are circumstances favoring price haggling.

3. A manufacturer's pricing sheet informs purchasers that they will receive a 10% discount from the total invoice price for all orders in excess of 100 units. This discount is a _____ discount.
    a) noncumulative quantity
    b) cumulative quantity
    c) functional
    d) cash

4. A manufacturer's pricing sheet informs purchasers that they will receive a 2% discount from the total invoice price if they pay their bill within 10 days from the invoice date. This discount is a _____ discount.
    a) noncumulative quantity
    b) cumulative quantity
    c) functional
    d) cash

Copyright © 1996 by Harcourt Brace & Company
All rights reserved.

5. The most widely used form of trade-oriented sales promotion is a(n) _____ allowance.
   a) off-invoice
   b) bill-back
   c) slotting
   d) discount

6. The jagged-shaped demand curve is associated with which form of psychological pricing?
   a) prestige pricing
   b) price lining
   c) loss-leader pricing
   d) odd pricing

7. FOB origin pricing means that
   a) the seller pays the transportation charges.
   b) the seller offers a discount based on the quantity purchased.
   c) the buyer pays the transportation charges.
   d) the buyer receives a discount based on the quantity purchased.

8. Which of the following is *not* an accurate statement about uniform delivered pricing?
   a) The seller charges all customers the same transportation costs.
   b) This form of geographic pricing is most appropriately used when retail prices are highly variable.
   c) Uniform delivered pricing is especially appropriate for nationally advertised products that have a suggested retail price.
   d) Greeting card companies use uniform delivered pricing.

Copyright © 1996 by Harcourt Brace & Company
All rights reserved.

9.	What geographic pricing practice is being used when a manufacturer charges the customer transportation costs that are determined from a competitor's shipping point rather than from the manufacturer's shipping point?
	a)	uniform delivered pricing
	b)	zone pricing
	c)	basing-point pricing
	d)	FOB origin pricing

10.	A company is considering bidding on a government contract to construct a new building. It estimates its cost at $2 million. It thinks it has a 0.7 probability of being awarded the contract if it bid $3 million for the contract. What is its expected profit?
	a)	$700,000
	b)	$1,000,000
	c)	$1,400,000
	d)	$2,100,000

Discussion Questions

1.	Windows 95, introduced in August 1995, was uniformly priced at $89.95 through advertising support agreements between Microsoft and retailers. Was uniform pricing a good decision or should Microsoft have encouraged retailers to set their own prices? Was $89.95 a good price, was it too high; was it too low?

2.	Price haggling is an American tradition when buying an automobile. Saturn has established a no-haggle pricing policy. Is this a good or a bad marketing move for Saturn? What are the advantages and disadvantages?

3.	Sam's Club is thought of as a deep discounter that sells merchandise in a warehouse setting. What factors allow Sam's to offer deep discounts? How successful is this concept now; how successful will it be in the future?

Copyright © 1996 by Harcourt Brace & Company
All rights reserved.

4. Airline customers must travel over the weekend to get a discount from most major airlines. What are the airlines' objectives for charging differential prices over the weekend?

Copyright © 1996 by Harcourt Brace & Company
All rights reserved.

Chapter 14

Promotion Management

Learning Objectives

1. Define the elements of the promotions mix.

2. Discuss the communications process.

3. Analyze the determinants of the promotions mix.

4. Define the promotions management process.

Chapter Summary

The product and its benefits must be communicated to consumers through marketing communications and the promotional element of the marketing mix. In today's highly competitive and dynamic marketing world, effective communications are critical to a company's success. Marketing communications represent the collection of all elements in an organization's marketing mix that facilitate exchanges by establishing shared meaning with the organization's customers or clients.

In marketing, promotion means to motivate—or move in a sense—customers to action. Promotion management employs a variety of tools for this purpose including personal selling, advertising, sales promotions, point-of-purchase communications, direct marketing communications, public relations, and sponsorship marketing. These elements along with the other communication elements in the marketing mix must be

Copyright © 1996 by Harcourt Brace & Company
All rights reserved.

treated as a unified whole, rather than as separable and independent activities.

For communications to be effective, a marketer must set objectives for the communications and follow an effective process of communicating the message. The marketer communicates either directly with the consumer or with the overall market. In communicating with a consumer, a marketer attempts to progress the consumer from unawareness to purchase. Regarding the overall market, all marketing communications efforts are aimed at building product category wants, creating brand awareness, enhancing attitudes, influencing intentions, and facilitating purchase. All communication processes involve a source, encoding, a message, a channel, a receiver, decoding, the possibility of noise, and feedback potential. Flawed efforts at any stage in the communication process will greatly reduce the odds of achieving the desired objectives.

Marketing managers have considerable discretion in determining which promotional elements to use and how much relative emphasis each should receive. Various factors such as the target market, product life-cycle stage, objectives, competitive activity, budget, and nature of the product all affect the promotional mix. The promotion management process includes determining the target market, specifying objectives, setting the budget, determining message and media strategies, and evaluating the results of the program.

Where historically many promotion and marketing communication decisions were treated as rather disparate and managed by independent departments that failed to carefully coordinate their activities, the current trend is toward integrated marketing communications, or IMC. Some key elements of IMC are that all marketing communication decisions start with the customer, which reflects the adoption of an outside-in mentality versus an inside-out position that historically has dominated this field. Another fundamental feature is that all communication elements must achieve synergy, or speak with a single voice.

Copyright © 1996 by Harcourt Brace & Company
All rights reserved.

The belief that successful marketing communications must build a relationship between the brand and the customer is another key IMC feature.

The adoption of an IMC mind set leads to several changes in the way marketing communications are practiced. Some of the changes include (1) reduced faith in mass-media advertising, (2) increased reliance on high target communication methods such as direct mail and Internet advertising, (3) increased demands imposed on marketing communications suppliers for full services, and (4) expanded efforts to assess the return on investment yielded by marketing communication activities.

Chapter Exercises

Exercise 1

During 1995 several manufacturers launched major introductions of new products. Ford Taurus and Windows 95 are two examples. Search a library (electronic if possible) for business publications of articles that describe the promotional campaigns of new product launches. For the examples given above, *Fortune*, *Business Week*, and *Advertising Age* carried articles describing the promotional campaigns.

Choose a new product and write a summary of the promotion that was used to launch it. Discuss the appropriateness of the manufacturer's strategy.

Exercise 2

Cycle Path Bicycle Shop has contacted and requested that you develop a promotional program for their line of Bianchi Hybrid bicycles. Following the Promotion Management Process, write a list of questions for the bike shop management to answer. Include guidelines for assisting the management in providing productive answers. The guidelines should, of course, be appropriate for marketing new bicycles.

Copyright © 1996 by Harcourt Brace & Company
All rights reserved.

Chapter Review Questions

(Correct answers are listed in Appendix B

1. Which of the following is *not* a promotion-mix element?
    a) personal selling
    b) sales promotions
    c) advertising
    d) pricing

2. Which of the following statements is *not* true for advertising?
    a) Advertising is a form of personal communications in the sense that most advertisements include pictures of people.
    b) Advertising includes both mass communication and direct-to-consumer communication.
    c) By definition, advertising is paid for by an identified sponsor.
    d) Advertising is not equivalent to publicity.

3. Which statement is most true regarding sales promotions?
    a) Sales promotions represent advertising undertaken by retailers.
    b) Sales promotions are a form of sponsorship marketing.
    c) Sales promotions are directed either at the trade or to ultimate customers.
    d) Sales promotions are prohibitively expensive for most firms.

4. Which of the following is *not* a key aspect of integrated marketing communications?
    a) It is critical that all marketing communication decisions be integrated with production and engineering capabilities.

Copyright © 1996 by Harcourt Brace & Company
All rights reserved.

b)   All marketing communications decisions should start with the customer.

c)   The promotion-mix elements should all speak with a single voice.

d)   Efforts should be made to build long-term relations with customers.

5.   When an IMC mind set is adopted, which of the following changes is *un*likely to occur?

a)   Mass-media advertising will increase in importance.

b)   Mass-media advertising will diminish in importance.

c)   There is likely to be an increased reliance on highly targeted communications methods.

d)   Greater demands are imposed on marketing communications suppliers to offer a fuller range of services.

6.   Which of the following marketing objectives is also known as creating primary demand?

a)   Building product category wants

b)   Creating brand awareness

c)   Enhancing attitudes and influencing intentions

d)   Facilitating purchase

7.   When a communications source puts thoughts into symbolic form, this is called

a)   decoding.

b)   encoding.

c)   recording.

d)   signing.

8.   Which of the following statements is true regarding the communications process?

a)   All communications involve, at minimum, a source and a receiver.

123

Copyright © 1996 by Harcourt Brace & Company
All rights reserved.

b) Feedback occurs at all stages of the communications process.
c) Noise is present only at the decoding stage of the process.
d) The communications process applies to advertising but not to other promotion-mix elements such as sales promotions.

9. A manufacturer's _____ strategy involves utilizing aggressive trade allowances and personal selling efforts to obtain distribution through wholesalers and retailers.
   a) IMC
   b) pull
   c) push
   d) encoding

10. A manufacturer's _____ strategy involves heavy advertising to encourage customer demand for the product.
    a) IMC
    b) pull
    c) push
    d) decoding

11. Which of the following is the best marketing communications objective?
    a) Increase brand awareness in 1997.
    b) Increase sales volume in 1997.
    c) Increase consumer attitudes in 1997.
    d) None of the above are good objectives.

12. Which is the most frequently used budgeting approach, especially in firms where marketing-department influence is high?
    a) top-down budgeting (TD)
    b) bottom-up budgeting (BU)
    c) BUTD budgeting

Copyright © 1996 by Harcourt Brace & Company
All rights reserved.

13.   In terms of specific methods for promotion budgeting,
       which is the most popular?
       a)   objective-and-task method
       b)   competitive parity method
       c)   percentage-of-sales method
       d)   spend-what-remains method

14.   A firm uses the percentage-of-sales method for allocating
       money to its promotional budget. With last year's sales at
       $10 million and next year's sales expected to grow by
       20%, how much will the company invest in promotion
       next year it allocates 5% of sales to promotion?
       a) $2,000,000
       b) $2,400,000
       c) $500,00
       d) $600,000

Discussion Questions

1. Recall to mind a popular consumer brand that is frequently
    advertised on television (e.g., Coke, Toyota, or Gillette).
    What are advertisers' objectives for this costly and extensive
    promotion?

2. An advertiser is dismayed when the message that a consumer
    receives from a carefully planned advertisement is entirely
    different from the advertiser's intentions. What factors
    (noise) can lead to this undesirable outcome?

3. Discuss methods that an advertiser can use to establish
    feedback for determining whether an advertising campaign is
    working effectively.

4. A manufacturer of a popular washing detergent decided to
    change the emphasis of its promotioanal strategy from pull to
    push. What promotional mix changes should the
    manufacturer adopt? Develop two promotional mix budgets,
    using percentage figures only, showing the old budget and the
    new budget.

Copyright © 1996 by Harcourt Brace & Company
All rights reserved.

Chapter 15

Advertising and Sales Promotion

Learning Objectives

1. Define the advertising management process.

2. Discuss the various forms of budgeting for advertising.

3. Define effective techniques and tactics of advertising.

4. Analyze the process of media selection.

5. Define public relations.

6. Discuss direct marketing communications.

7. Define sales promotion strategies.

8. Analyze point-of-purchase strategies.

9. Discuss sponsorship marketing.

Chapter Summary

This chapter discusses six elements of the promotion mix: advertising, publicity and public relations, direct marketing communications, sales promotions, point-of-purchase communications, and sponsorship marketing. Although each are treated in relative isolation, the importance of integrating the various elements—so that they speak with a single, unified voice—is emphasized throughout.

Copyright © 1996 by Harcourt Brace & Company
All rights reserved.

Advertising is a critical aspect of business, especially in the United States, where annual expenditures in 1994 alone were approximately $147 billion. Advertising is a valuable economic activity because it performs a variety of critical communications functions: It informs, persuades, reminds, adds value, and assists other company efforts.

The advertising management process consists primarily, of advertising strategy which extends from a company's overall marketing strategy, strategy implementation, and efforts to assess effectiveness. Advertising strategy, the guts of the process, entails four major activities: setting objectives, budgeting, developing a message strategy, and undertaking a media strategy.

Public relations, or PR, is the aspect of promotion management uniquely suited to fostering *goodwill* between a company and its various publics. Public relations involves interactions with multiple publics (e.g., government, stockholders), but emphasis in this chapter is limited to the more narrow aspect of public relations involving an organization's interactions with customers. This marketing-oriented aspect of public relations is called marketing PR, or MPR for short. Marketing PR can be further delineated as involving either proactive or reactive public relations. Proactive MPR is another tool in addition to advertising, sales promotion, and personal selling for promoting a company's products and services. Its major role is for disseminating information about product introductions or revisions. Reactive MPR is undertaken as a result of external pressures and challenges brought by competitive actions, changes in consumer attitudes, changes in government policy, or other external influences. Reactive MPR typically deals with changes that have negative consequences for the organization, such as instances of product defects or failures.

Direct marketing is a major growth area in marketing and an important form of marketing communications. Direct marketing is accomplished using (1) direct-response advertising, (2) direct mail (including catalogs), (3) telemarketing, and (4) direct selling

Copyright © 1996 by Harcourt Brace & Company
All rights reserved.

(e.g., home visits via Tupperware and Avon salespeople), although discussion in this chapter is restricted to direct-response advertising and direct mail. Database marketing, the computer storage and retrieval of huge data files, is the cornerstone of effective direct-response advertising. Database marketing has the virtues of addressability, measurability, flexibility, and accountability.

Sales promotion, the use of any incentive by a manufacturer to induce the trade (wholesalers and retailers) and/or consumers to buy a brand and to encourage the sales force to aggressively sell it, is an important element of the promotion mix for most businesses, especially consumer packaged goods. Consumer promotions (such as coupons, cents-off deals, premiums, and sweepstakes) and trade-oriented promotions (primarily off-invoice allowances to wholesalers and retailers) constituted, on average, 75% of businesses' promotional budgets in 1993, with media advertising receiving only 25% of the budget. Various factors account for the shift in the allocation of promotion budgets away from advertising (an above-the-line promotion) toward sales promotion and other forms of below-the-line promotions: (1) balance of power transfer; (2) increased brand parity and price sensitivity; (3) reduced brand loyalty; (4) splintering of the mass market and reduced media effectiveness; (5) short-term orientation and corporate reward structures; and (6) trade and consumer responsiveness. Sales promotions are particularly useful for purposes of introducing new or revised products to the trade, obtaining trial purchases from consumers, and enhancing repeat purchasing; however, sales promotions cannot makeup for inadequate personal selling or advertising, give the trade or consumers any long-term reason for buying a product, or permanently stop an established product's declining sales trend.

Trade-oriented sales promotions consist primarily of various forms of discounts, or deals, offered to wholesalers and retailers. These include off-invoice and bill-back allowances, and, in the case of new product introductions, slotting allowances to obtain

129

Copyright © 1996 by Harcourt Brace & Company
All rights reserved.

retail distribution. Pernicious aspects of trade promotions from the manufacturer's perspective include forward buying and diverting. The practice of everyday low pricing, EDLP(M), was introduced by Procter & Gamble to offset these practices.

Consumer-oriented promotions have as their objective obtaining consumer trial, holding or loading consumer franchises, and reinforcing brand images. Devices such as coupons, samples, premiums, bonus packs, sweepstakes, and contests, are used to achieve different objectives and accomplish these objectives by offering consumers either immediate or delayed rewards.

Communication at the point of purchase is another major growth area in marketing. Point-of-purchase materials provide a useful service for all participants in the marketing process. P-O-P communications also serve as the capstone for an integrated marketing-communications program. P-O-P materials perform four important marketing functions: informing, reminding, encouraging, and merchandising products.

One of the fastest growing aspects of marketing and marketing communication is the practice of corporate sponsorships. Corporate expenditures on sponsorships exceeded $4 billion in 1994 and are increasing at about 15% per year. Sponsorships take two forms: event sponsorships such as sporting events and recreational events and cause sponsorships. Event marketing is growing rapidly because it provides companies alternatives to the cluttered mass media, an ability to segment on a local or regional basis, and opportunities for reaching narrow lifestyle groups whose consumption behavior can be linked with the local event. Cause-related marketing, a form of corporate philanthropy with benefits accruing to the sponsoring company, is based on the idea that a company will contribute to a cause every time the customer undertakes some action. In addition to helping worthy causes, corporations satisfy their own tactical and strategic objectives when undertaking cause-related efforts. By supporting a deserving cause, a company can enhance its corporate or brand

Copyright © 1996 by Harcourt Brace & Company
All rights reserved.

image, generate incremental sales, increase brand awareness, broaden its customer base, and reach new market segments.

Chapter Exercises

Exercise 1

The hierarchy-of-effects model exhibits that consumers progress through stages of familiarity with a product before a purchase is actually made. A well-designed print ad facilitates this progression. Search through current magazines and clip or copy three or four eye-catching ads. Analyze the ads in terms of the hierarchy-of-effects model; determine whether the ad guides the reader from problem recognition to problem solution through the use of the advertised product. Write a review for each of the ads.

Exercise 2

In 1996 sales for Coca-Cola's fruit flavored drink, Fruitopia, are below company projections. Your task—develop a coordinated promotional program to run during the spring and early summer months to increase market share and sales for this brand. Your program may include elements of advertising, public relations, direct marketing, sales promotion, point-of-purchase and/or sponsorship marketing. Write a proposal that incorporates the five steps of the promotion management process (budget figures in percentages only).

Chapter Review Questions

(Correct answers are listed in Appendix B.)

1. Total annual advertising expenditures in 1994 in the United States were approximately
   a) $500 million.
   b) $500 billion.
   c) $145 billion.
   d) $47 billion.

Copyright © 1996 by Harcourt Brace & Company
All rights reserved.

2.	Which of the following is *not* a major reason for setting advertising objectives?
	a)	To force management to agree upon the course advertising should take.
	b)	To prevent advertising form being dominated by sales promotion.
	c)	To guide the budgeting, message strategy, and media strategy activities.
	d)	To provide standards against which results can be measured.

3.	The optimal (i.e., profit maximizing) level of an advertising budget occurs at the point where
	a)	MR=MC.
	b)	MR>MC.
	c)	MR<MC.
	d)	TR>TC.

4.	Assume that 40% of all U.S. households tuned into the 1995 superbowl football game. This figure, 40%, in advertising-media language is called a(n)
	a)	gross rating point.
	b)	rating.
	c)	market share.
	d)	audience.

5.	A certain magazine is read by 10,000,000 people. An advertiser pays $125,000 for a single, four-color page in this magazine. The cost-per-thousand (CPM) is
	a)	$0.0125.
	b)	$80.00.
	c)	$12.50.
	d)	None of the above.

6.	Which of the following is *not* a strength of television advertising?
	a)	high reach potential

Copyright © 1996 by Harcourt Brace & Company
All rights reserved.

b)   attain rapid awareness
c)   intrusive
d)   upscale audience profile

7.   Which of the following is *not* a weakness of newspaper advertising?
     a)   poor geographic flexibility
     b)   high out-of-picket costs for national buys
     c)   not intrusive
     d)   cluttered ad environment

8.   Which of the following terms has absolutely no relation with single-source systems for assessing advertising effectiveness?
     a)   Split-cable television
     b)   Optical scanners
     c)   Burke day-after recall
     d)   BehaviorScan

9.   Proactive marketing PR is
     a)   an offensively oriented form of publicity aimed at customers.
     b)   a defensively oriented form of publicity aimed at customers.
     c)   a publicity method directed primarily at communicating with stockholders.
     d)   publicity method directed primarily at communicating with government officials.

10.   _____ is undertaken as a result of external pressures and challenges brought by competitive actions, changes in consumer attitudes, changes in government policy, or other external influences.
     a)   proactive MPR
     b)   publicity
     c)   public relations
     d)   reactive MPR

Copyright © 1996 by Harcourt Brace & Company
All rights reserved.

11. Which of the following is *not* one of the distinct abilities of database marketing?
   a) factorability
   b) addressability
   c) measurability
   d) accountability

12. Which of the following is a correct statement about direct-mail advertising?
   a) It is more wasteful than mass media.
   b) It is less expensive on a cost-per-thousand basis than, say, television advertising.
   c) Its CPM is more expensive than mass media.
   d) It is inappropriate for use by business-to-business marketers.

13. Four factors account for the trend toward widespread use of direct mail by all types of marketers. Which of the following is not one of them?
   a) Increased cost of TV advertising and audience fragmentation.
   b) Direct mail enables measurable advertising results.
   c) Direct mail enables unparalleled targeting of messages to desired prospects.
   d) All of the above factors account for the widespread use of direct mail.

14. Which of the following is considered an above-the-line expenditure?
   a) advertising
   b) sales promotion
   c) event sponsorship
   d) point-of-purchase communications

Copyright © 1996 by Harcourt Brace & Company
All rights reserved.

15. The biggest chunk of the promotional mix for most consumers brands goes to
    a) advertising.
    b) consumer-oriented sales promotions.
    c) sponsorships.
    d) trade-oriented sales promotions.

16. Which of the following is *not* one of the factors giving rise to growth of sales promotions?
    a) balance of power transfer
    b) reduced brand loyalty
    c) corporate reward structures supporting a long-term orientation
    d) increased brand parity and price sensitivity

17. Sales promotions can accomplish all of the following tasks except
    a) increase product usage by loading consumers.
    b) compensate for a poorly trained sales force.
    c) encourage repeat purchases.
    d) stimulate sales force enthusiasm.

18. A large retail chain purchases chicken noodle soup from Campbell's Soup only when Campbell's offers an off-invoice allowance. The retail chain is engaging in
    a) forward buying.
    b) diverting.
    c) bridge buying.
    d) More than one of the above is correct.

19. A retailer receives credit in the form of a _____ from a manufacturer after the retailer merchandises the manufacturer's brand on a special display.
    a) off-invoice allowance
    b) slotting allowance
    c) bill-back allowance
    d) trade allowance

Copyright © 1996 by Harcourt Brace & Company
All rights reserved.

20.	A form of marketing-based corporate philanthropy is
   a)	sponsorship marketing.
   b)	event marketing.
   c)	corporate gift giving.
   d)	Cause related marketing.

Discussion Questions

1. Marketers generally feel that money spent on advertising is an investment in their company and in company brands. Explain the value of advertising that leads marketers to this conclusion.

2. The pink bunny campaign for Energizer batteries is easily remembered by many consumers. What features of this campaign make it memorable?

3. What interrelated activities must be accomplished to establish a successful media strategy?

4. The marketing manager for Limited, Inc., a women's clothing chain, has turned to an advertising campaign to bolster sagging store sales. What are the strengths and weaknesses of using television for this campaign?

Copyright © 1996 by Harcourt Brace & Company
All rights reserved.

Chapter 16

Personal Selling and Sales Management

Learning Objectives

1. Define selling activities.

2. Discuss characteristics of successful salespeople.

3. Analyze the steps in the personal selling process.

4. Discuss the basic functions of sales management.

5. Analyze the methods of organizing the sales functions.

6. Discuss the methods of sales force compensation.

Chapter Summary

Personal selling is a form of person-to-person communications in which a salesperson works with prospective buyers and attempts to influence their purchase in the direction of his or her company's products or services. The degree to which personal selling is used by a company in its promotional mix depends on the product, selling costs, customers' needs, and customer locations.

The field of sales offers many exciting job opportunities because of the job freedom, variety and challenge, opportunities for

Copyright © 1996 by Harcourt Brace & Company
All rights reserved.

advancement, and the attractive compensation and nonfinancial rewards that go along with sales.

The primary purposes of personal selling are to educate customers, provide product usage and marketing assistance, and provide after-sale service and support to buyers. All selling jobs, regardless of the product being sold, include the following activities: selling, working with orders, servicing the product, information management, servicing the account, attending conferences/meetings, training/recruiting, entertaining, out-of-town travel, and working with distributors.

The three main types of sales jobs are order takers who monitor inventory levels and reorder product, order getters who actively search out accounts and buyers, and sales support positions who provide pre- and post-sale support to both the salesperson and the customer. More specific types of sales positions are trade selling, missionary selling, technical selling, new-business selling, retail selling, and telemarketing.

In order for the personal selling process to be effective, all salespeople must follow some basic steps which are prospecting, approach, sales presentation, overcoming objections, closing the sale and follow-up. The focus in personal selling today is on partner-oriented selling since firms now realized that their own success depends on their customers' successes. This modern selling philosophy is based on trust and mutual agreement, a customer-driven atmosphere, getting the order *and* providing service, and maintaining professionalism and integrity.

A salesperson who has achieved excellence in selling makes a good first impression, has a depth and breadth of knowledge, adapts well, is sensitive, enthusiastic, has self-esteem, extended focus and a sense of humor, is creative, takes risks, and possesses a sense of honesty and ethics.

Sales management involves sales planning (the process of establishing a broad set of goals, policies, and procedures for achieving objectives), organizing the sales function (by

138

Copyright © 1996 by Harcourt Brace & Company
All rights reserved.

establishing sales organizations structured geographically, by product types, by market or customer classes, or by function), staffing the sales function (including recruiting salespeople and interviewing, testing, and hiring them), directing the sales force (via training and motivating), and evaluating and controlling sales force performance and satisfaction.

Chapter Exercises

Exercise 1

List the types of sales jobs that are presented in the *Specific Types of Sales Jobs* section of this chapter. Write a job description for each sales-job type. Indicate whether you would be willing to take one of these types as a first job out of college. Provide your rationale for each decision.

Exercise 2

To learn about the sales management function, contact a salesperson and ask for a 10 to 15 minute interview for help with a class project. Conduct the interview in person if possible, otherwise by phone.

During the interview, ask questions to obtain information about your contact's company in the following areas: 1) how are sales territories organized? 2) what type and amount of training is offered? 3) what type of compensation package is offered, (e.g., straight salary, commission plan)? and 4) how is performance evaluated?

Write a report of your findings.

Chapter Review Questions

(Correct answers are listed in Appendix B.)

1. A salesperson who calls on retail stores and handles inventory control, stocks shelves, or sets up point of purchase displays is
   a) working with orders.

139

Copyright © 1996 by Harcourt Brace & Company
All rights reserved.

b)   servicing the account.

c)   engaged in missionary selling.

d)   engaged in new business selling.

2.   Which of the following is *not* true of personal selling?

     a)   It is person-to-person interaction.

     b)   It educates customers.

     c)   It provides product-usage and marketing assistance.

     d)   It usually is a highly structured job.

3.   Which one of the following is *least* true of personal selling?

     a)   It enables a relatively high level of customer attention.

     b)   It yields more immediate feedback than any other form of marketing communications.

     c)   It is more efficient in terms of the ratio of cost to results than any other form of marketing communications.

     d)   It allows the sales person to customize the message to the customer's specific interest and needs.

4.   Which item is *not* characteristic of field sales?

     a)   job freedom

     b)   structured supervision

     c)   variety and challenge

     d)   advancement opportunity

5.   Which of these is *not* a characteristic of modern selling practice?

     a)   spirit of trust and mutual agreement

     b)   customer-driven atmosphere

     c)   seller-centered marketing

     d)   a solution customized to each problem

Copyright © 1996 by Harcourt Brace & Company
All rights reserved.

6. Brad works for Johnson & Johnson. He sells to grocery and drug stores and spends most of his time servicing accounts and providing customers with advertising and sales-promotion assistance. Brad's sales job would be classified as
    a) retail selling.
    b) new business selling.
    c) technical selling.
    d) trade selling.

7. Nearly two-thirds of pharmaceutical sales to retailers are through wholesalers. The wholesaler is the pharmaceutical manufacturer's direct customer. When the manufacturer's sales representative calls on retail pharmacies, he or she is not trying to make a direct sale to the pharmacies but rather to create business for wholesaler customers. This form of selling is called
    a) missionary selling.
    b) retail selling.
    c) new business selling.
    d) technical selling.

8. The sales representatives for pharmaceutical companies are called
    a) pre-approach negotiators.
    b) detail reps.
    c) relational communicators.
    d) middlemen.

9. Regarding the various determinants of salesperson performance, which of the following is false?
    a) Skill level refers to salesperson's learned proficiency at performing selling tasks.
    b) Accurate role perceptions are a very important determinant of salesperson performance.
    c) Salesperson aptitude and skill level are the same thing.

141
Copyright © 1996 by Harcourt Brace & Company
All rights reserved.

d) Personal characteristics such as physical size and appearance are important determinants of salesperson performance.

10. The highest priority in modern selling philosophy is
   a) corporate success.
   b) customer satisfaction.
   c) the bottom line.
   d) treating customers the same way you would treat family members.

11. Which of the following is *not* part of modern selling philosophy?
   a) trust between seller and customer
   b) integrity
   c) adapting
   d) a customer-driven atmosphere

12. Robert, a smooth-talking salesman of the old-school variety, regularly sells different people the identical insurance policy, regardless of their individual needs. He would rather persuade them to buy the policy he feels comfortable selling rather than spend time to analyze each customer's unique needs. Robert is in violation of which tenet of modern selling philosophy?
   a) He is not a hard worker.
   b) He is uncaring.
   c) He prescribes before diagnosing.
   d) He doesn't know his product.

13. Which of the following is *not* one of the five basic functions that sales managers must perform?
   a) staffing
   b) adapting
   c) controlling
   d) organizing

Copyright © 1996 by Harcourt Brace & Company
All rights reserved.

14. The ideal situation in designing sales territories is to establish
    a) sales territories of varying degrees of potential.
    b) sales territories of equal potential with levels of work load proportionate to the salesperson's aptitude.
    c) sales territories of equal potential and equal work load.
    d) sales territories of equal geographic size and work load.

15. Probably the most common form of sales management organization is specialization by
    a) geographic territories.
    b) product types.
    c) customer classes.
    d) brand classes.

16. The financial plan that most sales managers use to motivate their sales force is
    a) the straight salary.
    b) the commission plan.
    c) the combination plan.
    d) the monitor plan.

17. The type of sales budgeting that allocates funds in detail to each cost center and requires sales management to forecast and account for each item is
    a) program budgeting.
    b) itemized budgeting.
    c) line-item budgeting.
    d) typical budgeting.

18. Sales training of new recruits, continuing education of existing personnel, and motivational and incentive plans for all sales personnel are involved in
    a) staffing.

143

Copyright © 1996 by Harcourt Brace & Company
All rights reserved.

b)   controlling.
c)   planning.
d)   directing.

Discussion Questions

1. Tom Browne has received an offer from Procter and Gamble to join their sales force. Uncertain about personal sales as a choice of a career, he has turned to you for advice. What are the attractive features and misconceptions of personal selling?

2. Dell Computers have traditionally sold their products to business and industry by direct marketing (phone orders). Dell's marketing manager is considering establishing a sales force to call on major industrial prospects. What are the advantages of this type of promotional strategy?

3. Discuss the general characteristics that a company might use to determine the level of a salesperson's performance.

4. What is meant by the "modern selling philosophy"?

Copyright © 1996 by Harcourt Brace & Company
All rights reserved.

Marketing Course Project

Marketing Plan

The Marketing Plan project applies the course material to an actual situation where students bridge the gap between the classroom and real-life practices. The project is developed by groups of approximately five students who work over the course of the term or semester. A company or organization is selected with the assistance of the course instructor.

Marketing plan worksheets are provided to assist the student groups in writing and presenting the marketing plan for the selected company or organization.

Each worksheet represents subjects covered in *Marketing: An Interactive Learning System*, SIMIS CD-ROM, and the associated material. The worksheets are organized in the sequence that the material is presented in the text. The course instructor may assign worksheet due dates that follow shortly after the material is presented in class.

Copyright © 1996 by Harcourt Brace & Company
All rights reserved.

Marketing Plan Worksheet

Worksheet 1

Environmental Analysis

List the external forces that affect your organization's ability to serve its target markets.

Competitive Forces

Economic Conditions

Technological Developments

Political/Legal Considerations

Social Forces

Copyright © 1996 by Harcourt Brace & Company
All rights reserved.

Marketing Plan Worksheet

Worksheet 2

Market Segmentation

Analyze your organization's market segmentation strategy by identifying the bases for segmentation and the organization's target markets. Then, analyze your organization's performance in each target market noting its market share and sales growth.

Market Segmentation Strategy

Market Segmentation Bases

Target Markets

Market Performance in Each Target Market

Copyright © 1996 by Harcourt Brace & Company
All rights reserved.

Marketing Plan Worksheet

Worksheet 3

Define your organization's mission and develop an organization chart. Use the BCG or GE matrix to conduct an organization or a product analysis. Complete a five year sales and profit history.

Organization Mission

Organization Chart

Organization or Product analysis

Five Year Sales & Profit History

Copyright © 1996 by Harcourt Brace & Company
All rights reserved.

Marketing Plan Worksheet

Worksheet 4

Conduct a SWOT Analysis of your organization. Suggest strategies that match strengths to opportunities and convert weaknesses and threats to strengths and opportunities.

SWOT Analysis

Internal Analysis

Strengths

Weaknesses

External Analysis

Opportunities

Threats

Copyright © 1996 by Harcourt Brace & Company
All rights reserved.

Marketing Plan Worksheet

Worksheet 5

Define the target markets for your organization. Develop the
marketing mix for each of the target markets.

Marketing Strategies: Target Market 1

Define Target Market

Marketing Mix

Product Strategies

Pricing Strategies

Promotion Strategies

Distribution Strategies

150

Copyright © 1996 by Harcourt Brace & Company
All rights reserved.

Marketing Strategies: Target Market 2

Define Target Market

Marketing Mix

Product Strategies

Pricing Strategies

Promotion Strategies

Distribution Strategies

Copyright © 1996 by Harcourt Brace & Company
All rights reserved.

Answers to Chapter Review Question

Chapter 1

1. c; 2. d; 3. a; 4. c; 5. a; 6. c; 7. a; 8. d; 9. b; 10. a; 11. d; 12. d; 13. c; 14. d; 15. b

Chapter 2

1. b 2. d; 3. c; 4. d; 5. b; 6. d; 7. a; 8. c; 9. b; 10. a; 11. a; 12. b; 13. d; 14. c; 15. a; 16. d; 17. c; 18. d; 19. d; 20. c; 21. c; 22. c; 23. b; 24. d; 25. c.

Chapter 3

1. c; 2. a; 3. d; 4. c; 5. a; 6. b; 7. d; 8. c; 9. a; 10. d. 11. a; 12. b; 13.d.

Chapter 4

1. c; 2. a; 3. c; 4. b; 5. a; 6. b; 7. d; 8. a; 9. c; 10. b; 11. d; 12. a; 13. c; 14. b; 15. d; 16. d; 17. c 18. c; 19. d; 20. c; 21. a; 22. c; 23. a.

Copyright © 1996 by Harcourt Brace & Company
All rights reserved.

Chapter 5

1. c; 2. d; 3. a; 4. a; 5. c; 6. b; 7. a; 8. b; 9. c; 10. d; 11. d; 12. c; 13. a; 14. b; 15. a.

Chapter 6

1. d; 2. d; 3. a. 4. c; 5. b; 6. d; 7. c; 8. b; 9. c; 10. c; 11. a; 12. b; 13. a; 14. d; 15. c.

Chapter 7

1. c; 2. a; 3. c; 4. a; 5. d; 6. d; 7. c; 8. b; 9. b; 10. b; 11. c; 12. b; 13. b; 14.a; 15. d.

Chapter 8

1. b; 2. a; 3. d; 4. b; 5. a; 6. c; 7. a; 8. c; 9. d; 10. a; 11. a; 12. c; 13. b; 14. c; 15. d; 16. a; 17. d; 18. c 19. d; 20. c; 21. c; 22. d.

Chapter 9

1. a; 2. c; 3. b; 4. d; 5. b; 6. a; 7. c; 8. d; 9. a; 10. d; 11. b; 12. b; 13. a; 14. b; 15. d; 16. a; 17. b; 18. a; 19. b; 20. c.

Chapter 10

1. a; 2. d; 3. c; 4.d; 5 .a; 6. b; 7. d; 8. b; 9. c; 10.b; 11. c; 12. b; 13. d; 14. b; 15. b; 16. a; 17. d.

Copyright © 1996 by Harcourt Brace & Company
All rights reserved.

Chapter 11

1. b; 2. a; 3. c; 4. d; 5. a; 6. d; 7. c; 8. a; 9. b; 10. c; 11. c; 12. d; 13. a; 14. a; 15. c; 16. b.

Chapter 12

1. c; 2. b; 3. c; 4. d; 5. b; 6. a; 7. d; 8. c; 9. c; 10. b; 11. b; 12. b; 13. a; 14. d; 15.c; 16. c; 17. c; 18. b.

Chapter 13

1. a; 2. d; 3. a; 4. d; 5. a; 6. d; 7. c; 8. b; 9. c; 10. a.

Chapter 14

1. d; 2. a; 3. c; 4. a; 5. a; 6. a; 7. b; 8. a; 9. c; 10. b; 11. d; 12. c; 13. a; 14. d.

Chapter 15

1. c; 2. b; 3. a; 4. b; 5. c; 6. d; 7. a; 8. c; 9. a; 10. d; 11. a; 12. c; 13. d; 14. a; 15. d; 16. c; 17. b; 18. d; 19. c; 20. d.

Chapter 16

1. b; 2. d; 3. c; 4. b; 5. c; 6. d; 7. a; 8. b; 9. c; 10. b; 11. c; 12. c; 13. b; 14. c; 15. a; 16. c; 17. c; 18. c.

Copyright © 1996 by Harcourt Brace & Company
All rights reserved.